Yes, My Love Muffin

A Collection of Humorous Columns
Written by Tami Jo Riedeman

Printed in *The Hinckley News*
From 2008 to 2011
Hinckley, Minnesota

To my sister Bev
love Ellen

KoodB Creations
P.O. Box 614
Sandstone, MN 55072
www.koodbcreations.com

ISBN 978-0-9847153-0-5

Printed in the United States by Morris Publishing®
3212 East Highway 30
Kearney, NE 68847
1-800-650-7888

Appreciation

The hardest part about putting a book together is finding the right words to thank those who have been an essential branch in the creation of the project.

There's no question the number one thank you goes to God; my Savior, Comforter and Provider.

For my husband David, your humor and inspiration bring smiles to people far beyond the Pine County borders. Thank you my love, for having big shoulders, literally and figuratively.

To my friend and editor at the Hinckley News, Ailene Croup; this book wouldn't exist without you. Many thanks for giving me the opportunity to learn and grow as a writer.

Dona Bakker, author and friend of thirty plus years; your radiant faith and support are a key element to why I do this. Thank you a million times over.

If there was room, all my family and friends would be listed by name. Hope you know I love and appreciate you all!

For Dorothy and Dawn

Table of Contents

2008

2009

2010

2011

2008

How much for the free cats?
March 27, 2008

It's No Secret.....

It's no secret that the term "Free Barn Kittens," does not really mean free. It means that for the first hours I held those adorable mouse catchers in my arms, there was no monetary cost.

Four months later though, my husband and I had invested enough money in the kittens to buy prom dresses for 32 high school girls.

Did you know that kitten diarrhea can last up to a year (so says the vet)? Or, that an accidental front leg amputation only occurs at 5 a.m. on Sunday morning?

Then there was the cost to make sure our "free" cats didn't produce more "free" cats.

Despite the misfortunes, I can honestly say we have a calico tripod cat that is better at rodent patrol than most four-legged felines.

And then there was....

"I'll give you my horses because they need a good home," said the woman to this devoted horse lover (that would be me).

Reminder – this is another phrase for "free."

One of the two horses she gave me died, but not before financing our veterinarian's Florida vacation. My husband and I were not neglectful of his care, the horse was just stupid and had a stupid accident. That's all there was to it.

When it came to my young Mustang colt from South Dakota, my husband once again made it known that he was not "free."

"Yes, he is," I insisted, "The place is giving him to me."

"Maybe so, but you still have to pay for the transportation to get him here."

"That doesn't count."

Hubby wasn't going to win that argument so he left the room to go put more hay in the feeder.

A year later, the "free" horse, also not known for high intelligence, had a serious accident requiring the amputation of a corner of his mouth. This time my veterinarian took her entire family to Bermuda.

Now, before you assume we are reckless in the manner we take care of our animals, I can produce dozens of witnesses that will testify otherwise. My husband and I will happily open our checkbook for a pet's medical condition before choosing the alternative.

We provide quality food, safe shelter, yearly vaccinations and unlimited love and attention to our pets. Their humorous antics and devotion are more than equal to what we can give to them.

Two weeks ago, somebody I know was looking to give away their goldfish. Before I could utter a response, my husband whipped out a strip of duct tape and plastered it across my mouth.

"What?" I tried to gesture, "they're only goldfish."

One good list deserves another
April 17, 2008

It's No Secret…..
To my family and friends that I am very appreciative of my husband's domestic handiwork. He lovingly helps around the house and prepares delicious meals. However, I am concerned he is morphing into a Benny Crocker.

I've decided there are a few minor issues I need to discuss with him. Call it fine tuning our marriage.
Please don't use "impossible to remove" adhesive tape to identify the contents in my glass bowls. I can clearly recognize red Jello and chocolate pudding.

A man may need his pickled eggs, but he can make them in his garage using a hot plate and cooler.

Please cook your deep fried homemade onion rings outside. Our home smelled like a McDonald's Restaurant for three days. I spent $25 on air fresheners.

Thank you for the beautiful Easter eggs, husband. Next time, please rinse the sink after you pour the dyes down the drain. Pink and turquoise don't match my kitchen décor.
I don't mind that you accidentally burnt supper. I have done it myself. Just please don't feed it to me, or the dog.

Beer does NOT go with everything.

Now, just a couple of things concerning household chores, Honey.

You are not allowed to put four loads of clothes in the washing machine all at the same time.

You are taller than me, you get the cobwebs down.

Whether you like it or not, our bed sheets will be changed far more often than when you were single.

A wet bath mat gets hung up for a reason.

An empty dishwasher means you can put dirty dishes in it to be washed.

I asked my husband what he thought about this article and he said he wanted to contribute to it.

"How exciting!" I thought, "That my spouse has more self improvements ideas for himself.

A mere five minutes later and he handed me a list; for me. All I can say is that I appreciate the fact it wasn't as long as mine.

Gorilla Glue is not the answer to all your problems.

Tell me before you plan to nail items to the floor. Most likely there is another solution available.

There is a good reason I throw away the novelty catalogs.

Letting the dog "talk" to me via phone is not really all that cute. The barking hurts my ears.

Taking out the trash means taking it all the way to the garbage can, not just to the front door.

It would mean a lot to me if you learned the difference between a wrench and a ratchet.

Finally, beer DOES go with everything.

Cab of semi no romantic rendezvous
May 1, 2008

It's No Secret.....
My husband David, is a long haul truck driver. Every week he makes a run from Minnesota to South Carolina or Alabama and back again.

When we were first married, I decided to ride along on one of his trips. What a romantic rendezvous it would be! We would be sharing a small cozy space, eat out every day and have each other's undivided attention.

Sounds good doesn't it? But that's not how it exactly added up on the score sheet. I knew a few miles down the highway my idea of a "road trip" was different from his.

The first issue needing immediate resolution concerned bathroom breaks. Over the years, David's bladder had become like a cast iron cooking pot. He only needed to empty it every couple of days. My bladder first screamed for relief 6 blocks out the first day. I just knew there wasn't going to be enough rest areas to get me through Minnesota, let alone to a destination 1500 miles and 3 days away.

My ever resourceful hubby had the solution. He cut off the top portion of a plastic milk jug and covered the rough edge with duct tape. He handed me a roll of toilet paper, a package of baby wipes and told me I was all set to go. I was on my own though, on learning how to balance myself over the jug going 65 miles per hour down the road.

The next issue we needed to agree on was food. A semi truck and trailer are rarely welcome in family restaurants or fast food parking lots. That leaves truck stops and the more unusual places large enough for big rigs. Two meals at a truck stop and I was ready to fast for the week. Tired of my loud hunger pains interrupting his concentration, David started looking for other alternatives. He found it in southern Alabama.

"Look," he said great enthusiasm as he pointed to a sign, "that small community center is having a potluck and it has an over-sized lot I can park in."

I stared at the sign advertising the menu; chicken and goat stew, pickled onions and poysenberry pie.

"What is poysenberry pie?" I asked, a hint a fear in my voice.

"I don't think it's supposed to be poysenberry, I'm pretty sure it's meant to say boysenberry. I bet they didn't have the letter "B" for the sign."

"Well, that doesn't matter; I refuse to eat goat stew and pickled onions. And I forbid you to eat them also."

"Why?"

"Because you sleep in the bunk above me and you should be able to figure that one out."

I also discovered on our trip, my husband had skills I was unaware of. One in particular was the ability to trim his toenails while driving. "Hmmmm," I thought to myself, "how can he manage to bring his feet close to his eyeballs, yet this same man is unable to bend over to pick his dirty socks off the floor?"

As I was contemplating this issue, I watched a house coming down the road. Not too uncommon an event except for one thing; there was a man sitting on the roof of it.
"Why do you think he's riding on the roof of that house?" I asked my street savvy sweetheart.

"To lift up the power lines so they don't get snagged on the house as they go under them," was the straight faced response.

"Really? Well, next time I travel with you, I want to pull our house behind the trailer. That way I'll have my own comfortable bed to sleep in, a kitchen for preparing food other than Cheese Whiz sandwiches and a toilet that doesn't rock to the rhythm of the highway."

David gave me a loving but patronizing look, "maybe you should spend your next week long vacation at home or at your parents."

"But honey, I want to be with you!"

Catch the big one on film
May 15, 2008

It's No Secret.....

That fishing is one of America's favorite past times, especially here in Minnesota. My husband, David, is no exception, fish scales race through his blood like a marathon runner towards the finish line. He has more fishing tackle than the warehouses of Cabela's and Gander Mountain combined. When he forgets my birthday or our anniversary, he figures a matching pair of lures in a jewelry box will satisfy my earring expectations. As long as they are studded with diamonds I don't care.

I enjoy fishing almost as much as my husband as long as we set a time limit. We will fish for 4 hours at a time or until I get bored, whichever comes first.

For years I've been hearing fish stories from David, his relatives and buddies. Photos are often involved with the tales, as well as, showing off their beady eyed, high gloss trophies mounted on the wall. Each fisherman has their beloved lake in which they swear the number of fish caught or the size of the fish succeeds that of what the Gordon Fisherman himself catches.

One thing the men in my husband's circle do agree on though, is that the REALLY big Walleye, Trout, Northern or Perch is found in Canada. Minnesota has over 10, 000 lakes and enough fish to feed Paul Bunyan's family three times a day, yet it is off to Canada my husband and I go to reel in the ultimate prize.

Canada was the beautiful wilderness I had envisioned. The cute cabin we stayed in was reminiscent of Little House on the Prairie and the lake shimmered before us like the side of a giant Panfish. The sunrises and sunsets were spectacular. I was so glad I had brought my camera.

Unfortunately, what was supposed to be the fishing trip of a life time did not turn out that way. The reason was mostly

9

because I had unrealistic expectations on the art of casting and reeling. Once my husband baited my hook, (no way I'm about to skewer another live creature on a hook) I tossed the fishing line into the water. Three minutes later I'm asking why there are no fish bending my pole.

"Have patience, dear," says my devoted spouse, "nobody sent out announcements to the fish that we were visiting." David's fishing experience far outweighed mine so I couldn't understand why the fish didn't jump into the boat. With years and years of netting those slimy creatures, he should have had his own cable TV fishing show. It was a complete puzzle to me why the men and woman in boats next to us were catching fish to be proud of, while we were not.

In total exasperation, my spouse tried to explain it clearly.

"Honey, every time you see a bird or mammal on the lake or near the shore, you tell me I have to make the boat go as fast as I can towards it so you can take pictures. It's hard to reel in anything when the fishing line barely touches the water. Plus racing across the water is also scary for the fish, other boaters and wildlife. Let the loons and moose come to you, everyone will be much happier."

"I don't see a moose purposely swimming out a mile from shore just to visit me. Besides, we've spent plenty of time fishing. The only decent catch has been a 27" Northern by you and a 5 pound Walleye by me. Where are the 30 pounders?"

A loud chuckle escaped from my spouse's mouth and he replied, "Honey, you're going to have to decide whether you want to take pictures or fish."

"I want to do both."

"You can, just not at the same time."

"How about if you hold my fishing pole too and then I'll be able to snap photos."

"Who will operate the boat motor?"

"You of course."

David sighed and looked towards the cooler, "Hand me a cold one please, sweetie."

10

One person's junk is another person's treasure, even if it makes no sense

May 29, 2008

It's No Secret…..

That I was elated when Pine County sponsored Junk Days for its residents. Finally, I could load up my husband's idea of used "treasures," haul them away and restore our landscape to its natural beauty.

As I tried to push a broken lawnmower onto the trailer, a pained expression developed on my husband David's face. "Are you okay?" I asked him, worried that the sauerkraut brats he had for lunch had decided to excavate new roads in his digestive system. He assured me his bodily functions were fine. What was bothering him was watching the dispersal of his lawnmower collection.

I tried to be kind as I explained to my beloved spouse that eight non-working lawnmowers were in direct violation of the code. David looked confused, then asked what code I was referring to. "The marriage code," I said, "I don't have time to explain it right now, but take my word for it, you don't want to mess it up."

Not wanting to be heartless, I told my hubby he could keep two of the lawnmowers as long as the machines had the genuine potential for actually being able to mow a lawn. David attempted to convince me he needed more than two grass cutters, but it didn't work.

This is the same man who has an extensive assortment of coolers. You know, the kind you put ice, food and beverages in when you travel somewhere. Unless your refrigerator dies in the middle of summer, there is no need for a dozen coolers. My husband also has several non working television sets. Again, I don't see him taking them apart to put together a new one.

As kindly as possible I told my spouse he did not need so many unusable objects taking up space that could be used for more important things, like my horse equipment. His rebuttal went something like this:

11

"You would have plenty of room in your own building if you didn't fill the shelves with those 60 plus creepy troll dolls you have and the 36 busted Japanese cameras. Let's not forget about your dresser drawer full of single earrings, necklaces with missing links and bracelets with no clasps."

The count was up to three sets each of useless articles and we both wanted to stand firm in our belief that it was all a precious commodity.

"So what did you plan to take to Junk Days?" I asked David.

"I'll take 2 cracked sinks, four broken fishing rods and the mangled frame of an outdoor swing, he said.

"My contribution will be a cushion less chair I'll never get time to reupholster, two broken mixers and my first and only welding project."

After our pitiful piles of discards were placed in the trailer, we stared at each other, both feeling a huge dose of embarrassment. Surely, we had more unnecessary objects that we could eliminate from our lives. Our eyes searched the corners and closets of our residence.

There in our loft, was the result of David and I wanting to start our "own" special traditions. Over the last six years we bought more holiday decorations than any one household needs. There were twenty six totes of Christmas items, eight totes of Halloween, four totes of Thanksgiving, four totes of Easter and one tote each of Valentine's Day, Fourth of July and St. Patrick's Day.

It was definitely time to get rid of the holiday embellishments that were fractured, had lost pieces or were just plain ugly.

The process of finding things to get rid of was starting to become challenging and fun. Then David came across my three boxes of various teen idol magazines from my high school days, and my zealous desire to get rid of stuff slowed down. He was headed for the trailer with the boxes when I told him that someday I'd have time to sit down and read them again.

12

He laughed as he questioned my true motivation in wanting to keep thirty year old magazines. As I scanned pages of young men who I pretended were my boyfriends, I mentioned the magazines brought back happy childhood memories.

"I'm pretty sure Bobby Sherman and David Cassidy are grandfathers by now," my husband said.

"It doesn't matter," I replied, "put the boxes of magazines back in the shed."

David sighed then announced, "As long as you're keeping those gossip rags, I'm going to keep my empty Skoal can collection."

I rolled my eyes as I told my mate that keeping smelly tobacco tins made no sense at all. David argued and said that the lingering odor in the containers reminded him of how much he used to enjoy chewing.

Then I reminded him of how much I used to enjoy being a size 5, but that I didn't keep my skinny pants.

Before my loving spouse could make a comment he would regret, his father Mike drove up and observed our trailer full of rejects.

"Hope you kids know that half the stuff you have loaded in the trailer the county will not accept for Junk Days," he said.

David chuckled as he started to unload boxes from the trailer labeled with his name.

"Put those boxes back on the trailer," I insisted, "We're going to the dumps after our trip to Junk Days."

"What if the dumps aren't open when we get there?" David asked.

"Then we'll sit and wait for it to open. Here," I slid one of his coolers to him, "Fill this with cold drinks and cups of JELL-O, it might be awhile."

Dad picked up stray critters in company car
June 19, 2008

It's No Secret…..

That my love for animals is attributed to a childhood full of delightful critters. There's rarely been a time in my life when a four footed mammal didn't inhabit my backyard.

During my junior and senior high school days, my dad worked for a foreign car maker as a service representative. His company vehicle was one of the first models of the Honda car. Its size was comparative to that of a covered butter dish on wheels.

To save time and money, my father took out the back seat of the Honda car, laid tarps on the floor and used this makeshift economy "trailer" to haul animals home. He would stop by the livestock auction on a return trip from a business trip and purchase some orphan creature in need of a home.

I can only imagine the stares he received while driving on the freeway. A handsome man in a business suit, the back windows of his car rolled down and the head of a calf, goat, baby donkey or pig hanging out.

While the fathers of other children received chocolates or snow globes, my sisters and I were given the responsibility to bottle feed drop calves or clean pig pens. Happily we wouldn't have wanted it any other way.

My mom once asked my dad why he brought home a (fill in your choice of animal here.) His reply, "because we didn't have one." Sounds reasonable to me.

The only "family member" I despised was Alvin the turkey. Somewhere in his pea size brain, he forgot he was a turkey and took on the attributes of a rooster. Every morning at 5 a.m. he was below my window gobbling at the top of his blue lungs. If that wasn't bad enough, he chased me every time I left the house to go to the barn. I could usually out run him but that didn't keep my Thanksgiving dream from showing up a few seconds later.

I spent months climbing from the top of the fence to a tree then onto the back of my horse. From there I could chase the old tom until he found a place to hide until the next time he saw me emerge from the house.

One day we noticed Alvin had a difficult time walking around. He had sustained a serious injury to one of his legs. I know I should have felt sorry for him. If it makes anyone feel better, I did give thanks as I bit into his drumstick.

My mom enjoyed most of the animals as us girls did, except for the goats. They had a tendency to eat her rose bushes. One day my mom stopped to visit our goat Snowball. As she bent over to pet him, he reached up and licked her neck. Okay, not a huge deal. Nothing soap and water can't fix. Small problem though, Snowball had just eaten a small batch of poison oak.

Ouch!

That ended that goat's plans for a retirement at our house. Back in the Honda car he went for a road trip to the auction.

As long as we're on the subject of goats, I must mention Meatball. Our miniature goat so named because of the strip around his belly accented by a single round brown spot. Meatball was a favorite fixture around our hobby farm until he decided it was way too much fun using car roofs for a trampoline.

Jumping on our cars was one thing, jumping on the roof of my dad's boss' car was quite another. Meatball also had had a nasty habit of eating pine branches then burping in your face. That crazy goat never outgrew his cuteness or his orneriness.

It is pure joy to relive the animal stories from my youth and there are enough tales to fill a healthy sized book; but it is just as much fun to giggle at the pets David and I own now. And when our animals are quiet, we laugh at each other.

16

Husband does not dress to kill, only maim
July 3, 2008

It's No Secret......

My husband David and I have different views concerning fashion. On one hand, he thinks I worry too much about outfits that match; on the other hand, I am the one responsible he isn't in public dressed in hole infested tomato red sweat pants and a neon yellow tank top.

I think I give my husband a wide leeway when it comes to what he wears. After all, I haven't thrown away his favorite 15 year old sweatshirt. The one with the missing collar, tattered sleeve cuffs and gash the size of the Grand Canyon across the front.

When he wants to eat in the local café clad in stained work clothes, I don't have a problem with that, I do it myself. But when he wanted to wear lime green wind pants to a friend's wedding, it took a lot of beer to bribe him not to do it.

When we first started dating, we talked about a few rules of clothing coordination. I bought David dress socks to match his dress pants. He still doesn't understand white tennis socks don't cut it. If I talk too much about matching belts and shoes, my spouse's frustration level begins to rise. It makes no sense to him that if you wear black shoes you should wear a black belt, same goes for brown shoes and belt. David loves to wear his cowboy hat which looks much better if he's wearing cowboy boots and not sandals.

"Can I wear cowboy boots without a cowboy hat?" he asks with hesitation in his voice.

"Of course honey, what a silly question," I respond. The next area of coordination David asked me about had to do with jackets and sweaters. I told him that discussion needed to wait until we had been married longer, like 20 years or more.

17

In defense of my awesome hubby, it probably wasn't fair to give a long list of fashion do's and don'ts to a former long time bachelor. After all, he was never arrested or disowned for attending family functions sporting camo pants and a bowling shirt.

His idea, though, of dressing up is a "Will Trade Wife for Tractor" T-shirt and only-worn-four-times-this-week pair of jeans.

We had to make a few adjustments to maintain harmony in our relationship. David now asks me lay out his clothes for the next day. I think I've gone overboard.

As far as what my significant other feels about my wardrobe, he thinks I should still be wearing the standard fashion of the 1950's; dresses, pearls, aprons and high heel shoes.

No, the reasons aren't for intimate moments or Halloween; he thinks that attire should be for everyday. I would slap the guy except he's just too darn cute. So I roll my eyes and iron the shirt he needs for the next day.

Leaf blower not just for yard work

July 17, 2008

It's No Secret…..

That my sweet husband David has what you might call, an unorthodox approach to cleaning. It involves using "tools" that most people do not.

Here's what happened when I tried to help David sweep out his shop. He told me to stand back and watch a faster way to remove floor debris. When he brought out the leaf blower, I ran for the house.

Sometime later, after the clouds of dust settled back on the floor, I asked my spouse about his method of cleaning.

"Where did you learn to do that?" I asked him suspiciously.

"It's a guy thing," David said.

"Hmmm, do I dare ask him how he vacuums a carpet?" I thought to myself.

He must have been reading my mind because without any prompting he continued to talk about quicker and more efficient ways to do things. I was starting to get worried.

"Every guy knows not to use a leaf blower in the house," David tells me. I was about to hug him when I realized he wasn't finished speaking. "You use an air compressor."

The grimace on my face must have been evident because my honey looked at me with an expression that clearly said, "What?"

The next time I saw David's father, I asked about the leaf blower and air compressor thing. I was told "it's a guy thing" and that leaf blowers also work great for blowing snow off the sidewalk. A word of advice passed on to me, don't use models that require extension cords. I'll keep that in mind next time I have the urge to marry electricity and liquid together.

I figured there were plenty of other unusual uses for the leaf blower and air compressor thing, so I started asking around. Men were more than happy to boast of their cleaning and other ideas. I was told that both the air compressor and leaf blower worked great for removing cobwebs and dusting ceiling fans.

Are you in a hurry and need to dry a shirt or pair of pants? The leaf blower comes in real handy. Is your air conditioner on the blink? An air compressor works great but only if you stand back 50 feet from the nozzle.

Just because I'm old fashioned and don't want to lose an eye or something, I'll stick to my can of Pledge and a broom. I'll let the guys detail the inside of their pick-ups with air compressors and play badminton with their leaf blowers.

It's the first sign of confusion
July 24, 2008

It's No Secret…..

My frustration level rises when it concerns traveling directions. It's not like I can't read the signs, it just gets a bit confusing when there are three roads named 25th Street.

Is that all the higher the idiot engineer could count? I venture to guess this is the same person who decided the sign announcing an upcoming road should be a ½ mile from the road itself. With that amount of distance to wait to turn, I forget where I'm going.

Then we have the sign that gives no warning at all until you are almost past it. I shouldn't be punished for an illegal 'U' turn.

Let's really dump the wheelbarrow over by having signs that give you two unrelated directions. I usually want to go one way or the other. It is really irritating when I think I'm headed north and all of a sudden a sign appears that says I'm going west. It would have been nice to have a neon flashing sign that announced, "We changed our minds, we decided this road should go another direction."

And there is something really wrong when several roads with different names and numbers have to share the same sign. I say give that engineer more fingers and toes to count on and a name book.

When it comes to sharing sign stories, I must pass on the one I heard about deer xing signs. It seems as though a very citified girl thought Minnesota put the signs up so the deer would know where to cross the road. Okay, even I'm not THAT confused when it comes to signs.

The sign I hate the most though, is the "rest area closed" one. Since when does it take three weeks to clean a bathroom?

David speaks:

There is a secret, my wife Tami is directionally challenged. If anyone needs to give directions to her it goes like this. Right is always North Left is always south just don't tell her to go east she might back up.

Needless to say when she leaves to go on one of her "journeys" I keep my cell phone close by.

Example: Tami going to the airport.

The first thing that happens is the BIG question, "How do I get there?" So, after thinking about how to get her there the easiest, I write down the directions. Get on 35 and go south to 35(E) stay south on 35(E) to 494 and go west it will be a right hand turn, then follow the signs into the airport.

Easy right?

WRONG!

Off she goes, after about a hour my phone rings. Guess who?

"I was thinking about these directions you gave my and don't I take 35(W)," she asks.

"You can," I said, "but the bridge is out, and there's a detour to get around it, just take 35(E)."

"Ok," she said, "but what's the (E) stand for?"

"East," I said.

"You told me to go south not east."

After I explained the difference between 35(E) and 35(W) she was convinced that she was going south and the right way.

We hang up. A short time later she calls back, do I take this 694, she asks.

"No, keep going south on 35(E) to 494," I said, "then go west it will be a right hand exit."

Confused she asks, "if I go right won't I be going north?"

And here is the secret to my happy marriage…

I said, "Yes, I believe you are right…. They must have printed the sign wrong."

There may be such a thing as too much chocolate
August 14, 2008

It's No Secret......

My favorite food group is chocolate and my husband's is not. Sure, he'll eat all the chocolate chip cookies I make (if he left any of the dough) but he doesn't like chocolate. Maybe I do have to hide my Junior Mints, but it's because my spouse doesn't like chocolate, right? As far as chocolate brownies and bars are concerned, our nonexistent invisible children eat them when I'm not home and David is.

Being the kind hearted man he is; David enjoys buying chocolate for me. He realizes it is a healthy and inexpensive alternative to more horses or diamonds. So, for Valentine's Day one year he bought me a very large chocolate bar. And, by large I mean a 10 pound solid hunk of milk chocolate. Please don't think I'm not grateful for the gift, I was, I am; but it was actually a little too big. Did I really say that?

I decided that even if I nibbled on that chunk of candy everyday for the rest of my life I still would only consume two thirds of it.

Solution: break the bar into smaller pieces and use it for baking. Good idea but not an easy task. I took a meat tenderizer to it; all it did was make gashes on it resembling bite marks from some small animal.

Next, I laid a towel on the candy bar and used a regular claw hammer on it. That method produced a few flying slivers which lodged themselves into my kitchen curtains, cupboards and light fixtures.

The solution was to stand at the top of a six foot ladder, drop the chocolate bar onto the cement shop floor and finish it off with a sledge hammer. It worked great! I now have 312 baggies of chocolate in my freezer.

Never one to give up on gifts for his wife, David came home with another chocolate delight for me; soda. Yes, chocolate carbonated soda. – a six pack of it. We offer all family and friends who enter our doorway to try it.

"It's interesting we tell them."

A chocolate story wouldn't be the same if it didn't involve Easter candy. I told my beloved husband I liked Cadbury Easter Eggs, especially the caramel ones. Lucky me, Menard's Home Improvement Center is having a close-out Easter sale.

David walks into the house after a Saturday morning trip to Menards with two grocery sacks of Cadbury Eggs, the regular ones with yellow yolks. Not one to be unappreciative, I put them in the freezer with the other bags of chipped chocolate. Every few days I take one of the Cadbury eggs and lay it on a tree branch hoping some unsuspecting avian mistakes it for one of its own. As long as the chocolate doesn't melt and drip down the side of the tree I can get by with pretending I'm eating the candy.

I must repeat myself when I say I really do appreciate David's kindness and thoughtfulness, he just needs a gentle nudge in the right sales aisle. I don't want him to quit bringing me chocolate surprises. Even if the item is not edible, I still love sweets from my sweet.

We make different decisions in our youth
August 28, 2008

It's No Secret.....

That the voyages one takes during their youth shapes who we become as adults. That explains it all.

During my youth when I was naïve and much more agile, I agreed to do things that I thought would be fun and impress the guys. Not stupid stuff like drugs or drinking. I choose to spend time with friends who explored old mines and panned for gold.

This may not have been highly unusual except I was often the mouse used for being the first one to "check it out." Of all the places we ventured into, the one most memorable was a hole in the ground not much bigger than a coffee can lid. Somebody peeked in the hole and exclaimed, "I think this leads to more tunnels!"

Between my sense of adventure and friends bribing me with chocolate, I ended up with a rope tied around my waist and a small candle in my hand. They stuffed me into the hole, and said "You're the only one skinny enough," as they lit my candle. And I believed them! Oh, what vanity.

"Now, crawl down a ways and see if the tunnel gets bigger. If the candle goes out then that means there is no more air," one of them said. "Thanks," I mumbled as I watched for creatures not accustomed to being on the surface of the earth.

Carefully I dragged my butt across sharp rocks looking for something besides unhappy spiders and eyes that glow in the dark. There wasn't any hidden treasure or other tunnel entrances, just darkness, dust and the thought that this was a good place to hide the dead bodies of friends.

A second incident that occurred during my junior high school days involved a misprint on a rodeo flyer. The local FFA was putting on a rodeo and I brought home an entry sheet.

Wild Cow Riding was the first event on the program. My dad and I laughed about it and thought it involved putting a dress on an old Holstein cow and riding her around milk cans.

25

Always one to want fun adventures for his kids, my father said he would pay my $5 entry fee if I would do it.

"Of course!" I said, not wanting my dad to think I was some kind of wimp.

The day arrives of the rodeo and my dad and I wander around behind the arena checking out the stock.

"Hey dad, those aren't cows, those are Angus bulls," I said, trying to sound brave.

"I don't think you should do this," he said, "It's not what I thought it would be."

I looked at Dad and then at the semi small bulls. "No, I'm doing it."

So I allowed myself to be tightly strapped to an unhappy live hamburger by several really drunk cowboys. I was the only girl in that event and I stayed on for four seconds. My mother sat in the grandstands with her eyes closed listening to the announcer beg the audience for lots of applause.

My hard landing was fairly uneventful except for all those cowboys running out to rescue me. That was sweet. I asked if I could ride again.

Suffering from photography diseases
September 11, 2008

It's No Secret…..
One of my favorite places to vacation is South Dakota.

I am enamored with taking wildlife photos, especially of buffalo. My camera shutter goes off so often it sounds like a helicopter rotor. I develop photography diseases like mountain goat madness, prairie dog desire, pronghorn passion and donkey delight. Animals can never be too close to my face or too far away to drive to.

Protests from my husband David go unheeded when I hear of a herd of something at the end of a fifteen mile dirt road. David worries about my obsession and always makes sure my life insurance is paid up before we enter the State Park.

I think buffalo are beautiful, majestic creatures and I constantly look for the opportunity to capture their uniqueness. I just don't worry about pointing a flash in their face.

Thankfully, I have a man who tries to find ways to protect me from serious harm. The first step is to maneuver our rental vehicle between me and any animal weighing more than jar of Cheez Wiz.

The second thing David does is make me wear animal face masks that he has purchased at the ranger stations. Guess he figures the critters would just think of me as a steroid- induced relative.

And, the third precaution involves cranking up the volume on the car audio system as it plays the theme song from Top Gun.

What I really want Custer State Park to do is set up a camera store at both its entrances, complete with photo developing and camera repair. I take more photos in a four-hour drive session than National Geographic does in a year. (Okay, not quite, but my family seems to think so.)

And maybe most of them aren't worth printing, but hey, I still don't like to wait until I get home to see them.

Unfortunately, it doesn't seem to matter how many years apart I make my trips to the Black Hills, at least one of my camera lenses breaks during every trip.

During our 2005 getaway to South Dakota my telephoto camera lens quit working during the middle of a close encounter with a massive male bison. I made my devoted husband immediately drive to Rapid City to buy me a new one. We then went back to Custer State Park so I could continue my pursuit for the ultimate buffalo profile.

Thank goodness for extended park passes. For this year's rendezvous, the same lens I bought 3 years ago quit the first day we were in South Dakota. Luckily, I had a spare, the one that pooped out in 2005 which we had fixed when we got home from the last trip.

Do I have only one camera? Heck no, but I need a camera with a telephoto lens for the really spiffy pictures. Vacations are expensive I tell David when he starts to moan about the cost of our trips. Just think of all the interesting memories we'll have to share with our grandkids someday.

"Honey," he says, "eight miles down the road is a man who raises buffalo. Couldn't you drive there and ask to take photos? Think of all the money we could save."

I roll my eyes at him and respond, "No dear, it's not the money, it's the adventure."

Money is the solution
September 25, 2008

It's No Secret.....

That when I drive in towns bigger than Hinckley, trouble is guaranteed to sit in the front seat of my vehicle like an old sack of fast food.

The purpose for my latest trip to the Twin Cities was to drop my son and his girlfriend off at the airport. Okay, I know how to get there and back home so I should be just fine. But first, my son and his girlfriend wanted to visit the Mall of America.

We ate, shopped then left the covered garage to go to the airport. Fifty feet out into the open I have a flat tire. I haven't had a flat tire in five years. It was not possible go back into covered parking because I was on a one-way street and I didn't think my car would make a U-turn. So I found the last space in the nearest exposed parking lot.

My son and I got out of the car to change the tire and it began to rain. No strike that, it didn't rain, water poured from the sky like someone in heaven had turned a faucet on me. Did I mention there was a lack of precipitation when we left the covered parking? With my chintzy umbrella I did my best to protect my son from the rain as he so graciously changed the tire. Fortunately he had a raincoat which helped him stay a bit drier, because the wind played with my umbrella like the mini straw ones you find in expensive fruity drinks; which at that time I wished I was drinking at least two. Since I left my brain at home that morning, I did not have a protective piece of outwear.

By the time the tire was changed and we were back in the car, I looked like I had taken a shower with my clothes on. Thank goodness for padded bras because I would never win a wet T shirt contest. We managed to get to the airport on time despite my donut tire being less inflated than Botox lips.

After leaving the airport I took the nearest exit and pulled into a service station. The surrounding parking lot was over flowing with taxi cab drivers that began circling me like vultures discovering fresh road kill. I quickly filled my whimpy wheel with seventy five cents worth of air and headed down the freeway at the high speed of 35 mph.

The next hour was spent on the cell phone talking to my husband (who I blamed for the situation even though it wasn't his fault) coordinating plans for me to go to the nearest dealer where we had purchased the original tires. That would be somewhere in Forest Lake.

Between the rain storm and being surrounded on all four sides by semi trucks, I couldn't see the exit signs. Therefore, I took a wrong turn and ended up in Wisconsin.

I finally arrived at my designation, reluctant to exit my car because the heater blasting away at 90 degrees felt really good. The tire service employee removed the flat tire from the back seat of my car and proceeded to fix it.

When he was finished, he came into the waiting room area and told his boss the job was complete. The man behind the counter asked me if I wanted my tire back on my car. I had already whined about my misfortune when I arrived at the tire dealership. "Was he kidding?" Why would I not want my fixed tire back on my car? Was he going to offer me a prize if I drove all the way to Sandstone on the donut tire. Wait a minute; I know why he was asking me that question, the man who had actually fixed my tire complained about the seat of my car being wet. I was sure he wanted more money because his butt got wet. "I'm sorry, next time I'll fold the front seat down and find a way to operate the vehicle from the back seat," I felt like shouting at him. It was inconceivable to me that paying to have a tire repaired did not include putting it back on the car. So I did what any wound up wet woman would do, I whipped out my checkbook and said, "Okay, how much do you need?"

Orange vest over bathrobe suitable wear in 'man cave'

October 23, 2008

It's No Secret.....

Hunting season is nearly upon us. Time for men to move from the macho scene of a couch, football on T.V. and potato chips to one of camouflage make-up, guns and sitting in the dark.

There is something about a set of antlers on the wall that cause men's muscles to ripple and their voice to lower a couple of octaves. My husband David is not immune to this contagious fever that produces deer jerky and venison stew.

According to my spouse though, his aging has had a powerful effect on where he folds up his body for a long stretch of time during three weeks in November.

Over the years, my better half's deer stand has evolved from a homemade, barely there frame to a something I'm tempted to take over for a craft room.

David told me his first deer stand consisted of a few two by fours and an old pillow. It was a balancing act to perch his bottom on a board no wider than his wrist.

He would spend two to three days at a time in the tree, packaged mini donuts in his pockets and a plastic thermos of coffee. It was a butt numbing experience that was heightened only by a good snow storm. This was "roughing it" at its best.

My husband's next deer stand was metal frame with a cup holder and seat cushion custom made by his grandma. David's diet now consisted of a McDonald's-to-go breakfast and a Styrofoam cup of gourmet coffee. When waiting for trophy deer to appear became boring, my spouse could walk in a circle in a two foot square area and listen to his Walkman.

As the years have progressed; four sides, windows, a roof and a staircase have been added to the deer stand. Electricity soon became a necessity for the deer stand and was installed along with satellite T.V.

A free remnant of three inch, olive green, shag carpet has made it possible for David to walk around barefoot while he peeks out the windows looking for the "big one."

I try not to laugh when I see my sweetie leave at 9 a.m. from our home to go hunting. He throws on a blaze orange vest over his pajamas and bathrobe, tucks a newspaper under one arm and his gun under the other. Ammunition jingles in his robe pocket.

If it isn't too damp outside he'll walk to the deer stand in his slippers; otherwise, he puts on his tennis shoes. His new coffee pot has a timer so coffee is waiting for him when he arrives at the deer stand. There is a mini refrigerator, hot plate and microwave to prepare eggs, pancakes and sausage. A color T.V. plays info commercials for chicken steamers and pimple reduction.

If my hubby was able to get cell phone reception he would be calling for pizza delivery at lunch time. Instead, he has to settle for a fried hamburger, pork and beans and a tube of raw cookie dough.

During my last visit to his "man cave," I noticed he had hung a string of plastic bass camper lights around the windows. Taped to the walls were ripped out magazine pages of bucks, bear, and wild boars. When deer season is over, I'll be hauling my craft supplies in to work on beneath the bass fish lights.

Never let hubby pick Halloween costumes
November 6, 2008

It's No Secret…..

My husband David and I enjoy the festivities of the Halloween holiday. I'm not sure if it has to do with the guilt-free feeling of eating all the candy we want, or watching children smile at our imitation cemetery; I'm pretty sure it's both.

Plus, it's the only time of the year I let David say I look spooky without smacking his arm.

This year my hubby decided his costume would be a giant Whoopee cushion. I told him it fit his personality and he agreed. Then he turned his attention to picking out my costume. It was a skimpy female pirate outfit in a size I hadn't worn since I was twelve.

"That's not going to fit me," I told my starry-eyed hubby.

"Sure it will, I'll even buy you a parrot to perch on your shoulder," David said with way too much enthusiasm. I asked if it was going to be a real one or a stuffed toy animal. "Whatever it takes to get you in this outfit," he said.

Since I had a few weeks before Halloween, I decided if I worked real hard at it, I could probably lose a few pounds and squeeze into an outfit that resembled an unemployed Vegas showgirl's dress.

While I was busy trying to figure out which days of the week I would allow myself to eat; my spouse was shopping for accessories to match my costume.

First he bought an eye patch, then a plastic sword and, finally fake press on fingernails with skull and crossbones on them. While I lamented about wearing a corset, David bought make-up for a fake mole on my face that he thought would look sexy.

As far as his costume was concerned, he could get by wearing his pajama bottoms and slippers. The only make-up required would be an over-sized fart cushion is pink blush to the face.

33

I seriously wondered if I could bribe my hubby with five lbs. of candy corn and trade costumes. A little elastic and he could use the pirate dress as a shirt.

For the second year in a row, our Halloween party seemed to be a success. Adults became jolly as they tasted a fine spirit punch and kids played among the headstones displaying their names. There was lots of fun, food and conversation with friends we hadn't seen in a long while. The only disappointment for me was David giving everyone a cursory glance at his costume then changing into comfortable sweat pants and tee shirt.

"That's not fair," I said to him, "you're supposed to wear your costume for the entire party."

"I can't," David replied, "it's too hot." I complained to him that my outfit was uncomfortable but it wouldn't be right to change since I was the host of the party. David's solution to me was to take the parrot off my shoulder and the patch off my eye.

Grrrr, next year I'm dressing up as a nagging housewife.

Smith and Wesson makes Thanksgiving cleanup a breeze
November 20, 2008

It's No Secret.....

That I'm not the most experienced person when it comes to preparing a Thanksgiving turkey.

My aversion to putting a handful of bread crumbs inside a dead bird stems from an experience I encountered about eighteen years ago.

My ex decided a wild turkey dinner would be the ideal way to impress my parents. Unknown to me, he shot the designated meal with a 12 gauge double 00 buckshot. This left only a shadow of a carcass in which to prepare for eating.

My ex also neglected to get too thorough with the feather plucking; the result being an unidentifiable mass resembling a large lump of dryer lint. The worst was yet to come though, as the ex neglected to gut the turkey.

When I sliced open what was left of the deflated bird, small smelly round objects that looked like rabbit poop spilled out (I was later told it was fermented berries.) Those were quickly followed by grass, bugs and buckshot pellets. I screamed, not expecting so many foreign objects in my food or on my kitchen counter.

After the initial shock of dealing with the avian invasion, I decided my parents, my ex and I were going to dine on mashed potatoes, green bean casserole and chicken nuggets.

I, then, had to deal with another mess after the holiday meal clean-up. My 1965 washing machine broke while doing a load of dish towels, aprons, cloth napkins, place mats and table clothes.

The washing machine tub, full of water, flooded the small porch connected to the house. I didn't know whether to cry or throw objects as I went to clean up the mess with a mop in one hand and bucket in the other.

Having pity on me, my dad went out to his car and returned with a handgun. I wasn't sure how an assassination of my washing machine would solve my problems; but hey, it couldn't get much worse.

To my delight, my resourceful father, instead, shot holes into the floor so the water could drain out. I was elated with his clever idea and thanked him many times over.

Turning to confront my ex, I informed him he was not allowed any pumpkin pie until two things happened; one, that he clean up the remaining mess on the porch, and two; that he promise me a new washing machine. "And," I insisted, "the next time you get the urge to provide a meal, you take the checkbook to the store instead of your shotgun into the woods."

Ear plugs necessity for aging concert goers
December 4, 2008

It's No Secret…..

That I just celebrated another birthday. By celebrate, I mean that I am grateful nobody put several decades of candles on a cake for me to blow out.

At my age, I don't care if my husband David wraps my present in a Wal Mart bag and hands me a sticky note with the words, "Happy BDay" written with a carpenter's pencil. But his enthusiasm for my approaching the AARP age is disturbing.

David has admitted he is looking forward to the senior discounts I will qualify for since his age is quite a bit younger than mine.

Fortunately, I feel much younger than I am; at least this is what I always thought until a few months ago.

This past summer David and I attended a rock concert. Not those modern, head banging groups formed in the last few years, but popular classic bands from the 1970's. My personal preference for music is usually anything but rock n' roll, however, there are a couple of groups whose tunes I enjoy listening to while cleaning house.

So, it was with giddy anticipation that David and I went to a Boston/Styx concert. It didn't take long though, to realize age had changed the way we felt about music associated with a loud volume.

I quickly dug a pair of fluorescent orange ear plugs out of my coat pocket and shoved them in my ears. It wasn't because the bands didn't sound good; they in fact, were excellent. But my hearing seems to have evolved into the stage where any sound louder than my husband's snore irritates my entire body. I also have a problem understanding the words. The songs sound more like a foreign language in a high speed mode. This made it difficult to sing along.

37

Rock music also affected my other four senses in unhappy ways. My eyesight was never that great to start with; another year older and now it's really bad.

Trying to read the tiny seat numbers printed on our tickets required a strong magnifying glass and bright flashlight, neither of which I had with me.

So, David found our seats while he teased me about being too vain to wear my regular eyeglasses. Hey, I'm not giving up everything in the youth category.

As for the sense involving feeling, my bones definitely protested against the cold July evening. How could I have possibly forgotten my long johns on such a beautiful summer night? While I pulled my jacket tighter around me, other middle aged women who could wear spandex and black leather, danced in the aisles showing off their tattoos. They may have been shoehorned into their outfits but at least their teeth weren't chattering.

I chose not to eat or drink during the concert; I didn't want to worry about standing in a bathroom line that extended into the parking lot. So the only "taste" during the concert was a splash of soda in my face from an excited fan who forgot to put his cup down before clapping. Thank goodness for the lemon scented moist towelettes in my purse.

Speaking of scents, my sense of smell was at full attention for the banquet of aftershave, perfume, sweat and spilled beer surrounding me. The only aroma missing was the illegal substance Willie Nelson is so fond of.

All in all, David and I enjoyed the performance but realized as we walked to our vehicle during the final concert song that the volume was just perfect from several hundred yards away.

2009

Pros and cons of the Christmas letter
January 1, 2009

It's No Secret.....

That my husband David and I disagree slightly on the subjects of Christmas gift cards and typed photo copied letters.

We both represent a portion of the American population that either loves or hates the two items listed above.

My reasoning for liking Christmas letters is this: I enjoy hearing about the lives of those I don't have time to talk to or visit. The letter writers don't have time to call or visit me either so it works out well. Letters let you brag, exaggerate, whine and show off blurry photos of cute pets, ugly kids and vacations you've already been on.

David thinks letters are impersonal, a sign of laziness and boring. He thinks I should devout my hour and a half of free time a week to handwriting in each of the 62 Christmas cards we send out each year.

I asked my adorable husband if he was going to help me write in the cards. He said "no" but that he would put the self-sticking return address labels and stamps on the envelopes.

What a pal.

As far as the gift cards are concerned, I love them! I never get them but I still love them. What a treat to go to a store I adore and bring home items I will actually use. Put a gift certificate in my Christmas stocking for Fleet Farm or a book store and I am one happy woman. No more presents that find themselves in the Goodwill bin or live in a basement corner never to be seen again.

Every year David asks me what I want for Christmas. I tell him, "a gift card to Ace Tack store or Barnes and Noble or even Wal Mart," I'm not that picky.

41

He hates the idea of not being able to drive from store to store and wander around for hours looking for something he has no idea I'll even like. It intrigues him to stand in line behind cranky grown-ups and children throwing fits.

I've come to believe David looks forward to agonizing over colors, sizes and finding the perfect gift only to discover it costs more than a set of tires for his semi.

I, on the other hand, know he dislikes gift cards so I buy him food, beer and tools. Items I know I can get at a grocery store if I need to.

The gift cards we give to family members I know are not only appreciated, but the recipients actually look forward to receiving them.

Usually the relatives get several gift cards from the same store every year. They make it a family outing when the holiday season is over to the favorite stores and have a blast picking out what they want.

I told David we could enjoy that same experience; even make a date out of it. He said that his idea of fun was not spending half a day in a store just for horses or a store where he watches me browse through books.

"What would I get out of it?" he asked.

"You'd get to spend the day with me, isn't that a good enough gift?" I replied with a holiday sugar smile.

Hard to find a bird that doesn't doo it
January 15, 2009

The next time a social event requires a step up in the grooming department, I will not nag my husband. It is not worth the exchange of words to try to get David not to look like ZZ Top.

I have decided for a New Year's goal not to insist my favorite man keep his shop clean, pick his socks up off the floor or snore during a movie.

Instead, I will focus on correcting those idiosyncrasies in my own life. Such as spending less money on hair color and horse equipment, fixing things better left alone and making fun of my adorable husband. Oh wait, that last one; that might be kind of tough, okay maybe impossible.

One of our more recent conversations involved David's plan to build a chicken coup and actually put chickens in it. "No way," I said, "the two of us don't eat enough eggs to justify the cost."

I continued on with a list of reasons NOT to have chickens; they smell really bad, David doesn't eat chicken (he's allergic to it), and there would be nobody to take care of them during the week because I refused to.

I asked my ambitious spouse why he wanted chickens. His answer, "just because." That's not enough reason for me.

As he explained in great detail how he planned to build a chicken coup in my front yard, I kept telling him "no." Finally, to end the conversation, I told him go ahead and build it. "Just remember," I said, "as soon as you leave on the road for the week, I'm going to leave the coop door open, let the chickens go where they want to, and put your gardening tools in the shed. Or, if the coup smell isn't too bad, I'll turn it into a tack room for all the horse equipment I plan to buy.

Hubby just stared at me for a moment then asked, "Can I have pheasants in the coup instead of chickens?"

43

I asked David if pheasants were as stinky as chickens. He didn't know so I told him let's not take a chance and not have a coup for anything.

After a few minutes of silence my "need-another-thing-to-do" husband spoke, "I think we need to get a couple of steers and a couple of pigs this summer."

I very calmly said, "Steers yes, pigs no." David sighed deeply and asked why. "Because," I replied, "pigs stink and I'm afraid they'll eat my kittens if they get too close."

He looked at me with disbelief then asked what meat source could we raise on our place.

"Fish; you could build me a waterfall and pond and we could put fish in it," I said with much excitement. David reminded me that neither one of us eat fish, especially goldfish.

"Oh, that doesn't matter Honey, at least they would be pretty to look at."

Treats: The secret to good behavior
January 29, 2009

The next time I am asked about my secret to training well behaved pets I will respond with one word, treats.

It doesn't matter if its apple flavored horse goodies, doggy bacon bits or in David's case, peanut butter cookies; treats are what makes my loved ones even more lovable.

Case in hand, I woke one morning last week to discover one of my four horses staring at me through a ground level window of my house. Hmmm, not good, last time I checked the horse border was a good hundred feet from the house.

I quickly put on a pair of boots and threw a jacket on over my P.J.s. As soon as I walked out the front door I was greeted by three more pairs of eyes. Okay, so all four horses are hanging out by the front door, no doubt waiting for their ritual morning treats and hugs.

I casually walked towards their pen; all four of them following me like a string of popcorn. They continued right into the pen without aid of halter, rope or whip. I fixed where the horses found their freedom, gave them a tasty goodie and left my four equine friends looking longingly at their "boarded" up escape route.

In regard to my dog, I give him a treat every morning after he takes his daily dose of thyroid medication. Believe it or not, my dog opens his mouth and swallows his pill without a bit of resistance. Of course the pill is the size of a mouse turd and that might have something to do with it too.

My adorable husband David isn't so easily taken in by edible temptations. Sure, I can convince him to clean the cat litter box with a pan of lemon bars; but even a three-layer carrot cake with cream cheese frosting will not entice my spouse to iron his own shirts.

We've only been married six years so I'm still learning the art of persuasion on a man who quickly learned that saying "yes" to me, even without a sweet, gives him grey hair and reasons to hide in his shop.

I guess it's important to share where I stand on this issue. As long as the morsel is chocolate I will do almost anything. There are lines I won't cross of course; those areas include illegal, immoral or anything requiring the use of a grease gun.

I wish I could say my four cats believe in the "treat for a favor" theory. They figured out long ago that to get what they want, they just need to wander into the kitchen, squeak out a soft meow and sit close to the counter where a cookie jar sits with kitty treats in it. I sure hope the day doesn't come where my husband studies cat behavior.

Stuck on spring
February 12, 2009

I am elated that spring is not a thousand miles away. One of several reasons for feeling this way is because I am tired of getting my husband unstuck.

There hasn't been one time when David has plowed our driveway with our tractor that he didn't slide off the driveway and bury the tractor up to its underbelly. It usually happens when I am trying to get ready for work.

This means hubby comes into the house when I am in the process making myself presentable and requests my help. I stop what I'm doing, put a layer of Carharts over my dress clothes and give myself hat hair by placing my bomber hat on my head. We hook the Suburban to the tractor, yell at each above the noise of diesel motors, and after a few hard pulls, the tractor is out.

On the average, these incidents take 15 to 20 minutes. Not a lifetime, but enough time to make me forget which make-up I put on and whether or not I brushed my teeth.

My intention is not to portray my spouse on the negative side; but he has been told to stay away from the driveway area that sucks him in like a two for one tool sale at a hardware store.

This spring I'm going to use David's fishing trip money to have that hole filled in with boulders.

A couple of weeks ago, my favorite man was using the tractor to push a large hay bale. The area around the bale was icy and thick with snow. David got the tractor stuck, managed to get it out and then re-stuck.

I left the project I was working on and helped him use the pick-up to get the tractor back to solid ground. I am beginning to wonder if there is something about getting stuck that makes my man enjoy his vehicles more or if the need exists to discover the limitations of horse power.

If the incidents listed above were my loved one's only misdemeanors then I shouldn't really complain.

47

However, just recently David was in his four-wheel-drive pickup and ended up getting it stuck in a two foot deep snow bank. There was a cleared area he could have turned around in, but apparently the white wet solidified substance was too tempting not to drive in.

Must be a guy thing. This time we used the tractor to pry the pick-up out of its predicament. I'm seeing a pattern here and it's not good. How do I get my otherwise intelligent husband to quit sinking wheels especially during the times I am legitimately busy? I really don't know the answer to my own question, so if you have a solution, contact me at the newspaper.

Most embarrassing moment makes
great tale for husband
February 26, 2009

The next time my husband David and myself walk out the front door, I must remember to look in the mirror one last time. If there is lipstick on my teeth, a smudge of chocolate on my face or my bra strap shows, my loving hubby will not tell me until after we have arrived back home. I've asked him why he doesn't say something before I give others the pleasure of silently laughing at me.

"I didn't notice," is what David's response is. "How can you not notice marks on my teeth that look like a set of red braces?" I ask.

His comeback is that because he is too busy looking at my beautiful face. Hmmm. Nice try Honey, but if you were really looking at my face then you couldn't miss the various times when my mascara dissolved into black teardrops on my cheeks or minty green toothpaste flecks looked like boogers on my upper lip.

I tell David that I let him know if he has an embarrassing issue that needs taking care of.

"I really don't care," he says.

"Yes you do," I reply, "I'm sure you'd like to know if icky things are in your mustache or a nose hair is longer than Rapunzel's braid."

This short conversation led to sharing other embarrassing moments. The standards were mentioned; forgetting a name, criticism of smoking in front of non-smokers and trying to open the door of the car that only looks like mine.

As I rattled off more humiliating incidents; inedible food dishes, vibrant clothing stains in inappropriate locations and sharing facts that weren't facts at all, David just smiled and kept quiet.

"My most embarrassing moment was when I was in the 7th grade," I continued. It was my first day in Jr. High School. I was wearing a bright red quilted coat and I had polished my gold rimmed glasses. There was a boy I hoped to impress enough for him to consider making me his girlfriend (incidentally, his name was David). I was standing in the courtyard talking to David (potential boyfriend) and his friend when a flock of squawking seagulls flew overhead. And yes, you guessed it; they pooped on the arm of my brand new jacket. Crap!

My mortification at that time is beyond description, even today. For the next three years at the jr. high I avoided the courtyard, David and wearing that red coat. My husband chuckled at my story, which I expected.

"Your turn," I said.

"For what?" David asked.

"Your most embarrassing moment," I replied.

He shrugged his shoulders, muttered something about not remembering one and headed towards the refrigerator.

"You're not getting off that easy," I said. I just revealed all kinds of embarrassing tidbits to you, now you need to share with me."

David winked at me and said, "I can't think of anything right now, but when I do, I'll let you know. By the way, thanks for giving me something new to share with the guys at coffee time." I watched my man sit down on the couch with a cold one and turn the T.V. on.

My evil eye went unnoticed and I decided my most humiliating time was yet to come. It would be when they put my mug shot in the newspaper for harming my hubby.

Men should know marriage isn't fifty-fifty
March 12, 2009

Last weekend my adorable husband David labeled himself "Mr. Wrong."

"Why are you doing that?" I asked.

"Because I always seem to be wrong," he replied.

"You aren't *always* wrong, only 75% of the time," I said.

"See, I'm even wrong about the amount of time I'm wrong," Hubby said as he let out an exaggerated sigh. I rolled my eyes and then we both laughed. I think David likes using the "Mr. Wrong" card to solicit sympathy.

"Poor picked on husband can't seem to catch a break."

Hmmm. I think he enjoys being a scrapegoat celebrity. I told my spouse there is an advantage to consistently being wrong.

"What is that?" David asked suspiciously. "You don't have to know the correct facts about everything," I said with a smile. I received a quizzical look so I continued to talk to my loved one about the role of being "Mr. Wrong."

By now David should realize that being "Mr. Wrong" is just part of the marriage package. It fits in the same category as "Yes Dear," Whatever you say Dear," "You are right Dear" and David's favorite, "Yes my love muffin, did I tell you you're beautiful today?"

Being slightly older than David lends credibility to my being right more than him.

"I've been around longer than you Honey," I say to my hubby, "I know these things."

The biggest subject we have a tendency to "disagree" about concerns David's recollection of phone conservations. At my hubby's insistence I call him when I get off work late at night. Its sweet he is concerned about my safety but he is usually in a very deep sleep when I call. So the discussion goes like this;

51

"Hello Honey," I say.

He answers in a groggy voice, "Hallo."

"I'm on my way home from work."

"Home? You want me to come get you?"

"No Dear, you're in Georgia, I'm fine and just going home."

Hubby's voice still sounding like a mouthful of Styrofoam popcorn David continues, "I'll be there in a minute, I have to finish plowing the field."

"Sweetie, go back to sleep, you don't know what you're saying. I'll talk to you in the morning."

There is a long silence before David finally says, "Okay" and hangs up.

The next morning I tease Hubby around the previous night's conversation. He of course, insists I am wrong and that he remembers clearly what he said. So I ask him that if he remembers so well, then why he was plowing a field in Georgia.

Once again, he claims he said no such thing. Since this same discussion takes place every week I change the topic and remind him one last time that he is wrong.

Now, lest you think I don't confess to being wrong myself, I do. It's just different for the wife. Men, just ask your wife, she's usually right.

It began with a few fish
April 2, 2009

Not long ago, people I saw ice fishing led me to thinking about summer fishing, which led me to thinking about the goldfish my husband David and I used to have.

It all started a couple weeks before we got married. Our future home had a small rock pond in the front yard and we decided a few goldfish in it would be a special feature for our outdoor reception.

Off to the pet store we went to purchase a couple dozen 12-cent goldfish. We bought so many figuring most of the fish wouldn't survive due to one reason or another. How wrong we were.

Even after a lucky catch or two from our cat, children at the reception fishing for them and a hungry crow, we still ended up with 17 of the 24 alive by the time fall arrived.

This presented a new problem for us; what to do with them before winter arrived. Fortunately, we found a used 60-gallon aquarium at a garage sale. Unfortunately, the tank was still too small for all 17 fish.

By the time the first few snowflakes fell, nine small fish were nine middle-sized fish. (The other eight went to fishy heaven.)

When the robins announced spring, all nine fish were tossed back into the pond. Not only did they increase in size, but some of them had baby fishies. Great, what are we going to do with all fish? You can't eat them and I couldn't bear the thought of flushing them down the white porcelain throne.

David and I had grown attached to the nine original fish but didn't want their off-spring.

Since I worked for a school district at the time; a fabulous idea came to mind. If students brought a note from home saying their parents gave them permission, the student could have free fish.

This idea became more popular than an open book test. The junior high age kids thought I actually bordered on the "cool" side. So, for a couple of weeks I hauled a minnow pail of fish to school. The students brought containers and loaded them up with baby goldfish to take back home.

When the novelty of free fish worn off at the school, we had a garage sale at our house; and gave more fish away. Buy something at the garage sale and get a free fish. Don't buy something at the garage sale and get a free fish.

Winter arrived on schedule and still goldfish overflowed at our home. To accommodate all of them, David bought a 100 gallon rubber water tank. We put the unit in our basement and moved the fish into their new home for the season.

For five years we continued a cycle of moving fish back and forth from pond to trough. The most unpleasant part of having fish was the continual cleaning of the tanks. Goldfish are dirty and do not have as short as life spans as people think.

Perhaps goldfish won at carnivals only last twelve hours; ours lasted longer than the nine lives of a cat.

As fate would have it, the summer we were planning on moving, all of the fish suddenly disappeared. One day half the fish were missing, the next day the other half vanished.

I don't know what happened to them; all I can say is "thank you" to whoever it was.

Although there are times I miss watching the graceful swimming and brilliant colors of the fish; I am glad I don't have to have a 100-gallon tank sitting in the middle of my living room; which is where it would probably have to be in my new home.

Hubby's wedding etiquette has
new version of dollar dance
April 23, 2009

After attending the beautiful wedding of a cousin this last weekend, I decided my husband David needed to be educated in the wedding etiquette department.

Although my spouse is a kind, considerate and wonderful human being, he lacks a little in the "flair" department.

First item on the list concerns grooming. Make sure hubby doesn't cut his own hair the night before the wedding. At 10:38 p.m. David wants to know what he can do with a hairstyle that belongs on Ringo Starr. Hmmm. Do I laugh at him or get mad and hide all my scissors? Probably both.

The next morning I handed David a to-go cup of coffee, a donut and told him not to come home until he found a barber and paid him to fix his hair.

During the wedding ceremony my hubby had a difficult time being quiet. When the minister mentioned "love and obey" "for richer or poorer" "till death do you part" David felt he should warn his male cousin that in marriage you usually didn't get much of part A, it was mostly part B.

Out of respect for the bride and groom, I didn't respond in the manner my husband deserved.

Then there is the subject of dancing. I know it isn't one of David's favorite pastimes, he'd rather clean the cat litter box than have to shake his hips in front of a couple hundred people.

At the reception, he stooped to a new low when he handed out dollar bills to nephews, new acquaintances and the catering van driver as bribes to dance with me. Even during the songs dedicated to husbands and wives I found myself slow dancing with a maintenance worker from the VFW hall.

As long as we're on the subject of dancing, I made a promise to myself not to ever wear another dress or skirt that has "twirl" potential.

While David enjoyed sitting at a table watching me dance, he took photos of me while my dress was half way to my ears. Not cool.

This type of behavior falls into the same category that will get my other half firm lectures from his mother and a slap on the back of the head from me.

David! It is an absolute no-no to give the bride bunny ears during family photos. Also not funny is writing "help me" on the groom's champagne glass or tying road kill to the newly married couple's car bumper.

When my spouse put a plate of wedding cake in front of me I was so appreciative; until I noticed the frosting around the edge of the cake was missing.

"Where's the frosting?" I asked David.

"I ate it," he replied.

I gave him squinted-eye stare and said to him in a firm voice." I hope you didn't scrap the frosting off the rest of the wedding cake."

David glanced at the wedding cake, then at me, stuffed a forkful of cake in his mouth and walked over to the DJ in charge of the music. He handed the guy a dollar bill while clearly making some kind of request. A few minutes later the song "I Love You Truly" played and I knew what David was trying to say, that he did eat the frosting around the wedding cake, but that he also did really love me.

Creative gardening style includes manure, beer cans, rutabagas
May 7, 2009

Spring brings orchestras from songbirds, carpets of green grass and a difference of opinion concerning a garden between me and my husband David.

I thought David's garden was just the right size for the time and energy he had to devote to it. So, I was quite surprised to come home from work one day and discover a portion of my horse pasture plowed up.

I questioned my hubby about my lost field of horse grass and where he was going to find the additional time to take care of a larger garden. His only response was, "I'm going to fill that area with rutabagas."

"You and I don't eat rutabagas'. In fact, we don't know anyone who does."

David gave me that "I know something you don't" look.

"What?" I said.

"I bought an antique rutabagas cutter at an auction today."

As usual, I gave my spouse the look that says, "What were you thinking?" I then proceeded to tell David that if I was losing horse pasture, he was going to plant that area in carrots; for my horses.

"What am I going to use the rutabagas cutter for if I can't have rutabagas?" David asked in his poor me tone of voice.

"We'll use it as a flower container," I replied.

A few minutes later I walked over to my other pasture to talk to my horses. The first thing I noticed as I made my way through the gate was a fifteen- foot high mound of manure and old hay. Now, David did a great job cleaning up the pasture and I really, really appreciated it; but, the pile was put in a place that everyone who comes over will notice immediately.

I talked to my darling about his choice of location for the manure mound and why he didn't put it somewhere less visible.

His answer, "I don't know, seemed like a good spot to me."

Grrrrrr.

I asked David why he didn't put at least some of the compost directly on his garden. Once again, his response was not one I wanted to hear; the compost was for next year's garden.

Grrrrrr again.

Deciding there is nothing I can do about the compost pile; I wander over to where my flower garden is. My plans include yard ornaments that look like sleeping fawns, shy squirrels and playful bear cubs. Unfortunately, my husband had a different vision for what should frolic among my blossoms. Dead center in my flower bed was a cracked toilet and a shepherd's hook holding a wind chime made of beer cans.

I knew for certain right then and there that asking David to build me a small rock waterfall for our deck would not be a good idea. First of all, he would probably use old rusty car parts instead of field stones to construct it. Second, the liquid flowing through it would not be clear fresh water.

I searched around our property looking for mushrooms that I believed my spouse must have tasted in order to have such unorthodox ideas in regards to our landscaping and gardens.

When I didn't find any mushrooms, I concluded David was thinking up these things on his own without any outside influences. Oh boy.

Beer can wind chime rattles gardener's cage
June 4, 2009

Not long ago, my kind considerate husband David was home all week due to our semi truck being broke down. I will be the first to admit my beloved deserved a week off. He works hard on the road during the week and when he comes home on weekends. There is a difference of opinion though, on how his time should be spent when he is at home. There seems to be an issue concerning balance.

Each day my honey bun does an exceptionally sweet thing for me, and then counters with something I could do without.

Day One of hubby being home: He designs and builds a pulley system for my bird feeders that hang on a ten-foot pole. Yeah! No more sunflower seeds down my shirt using the old system. The old design consisted of hanging the bird feeder on a board with nails in it, then lifting it beyond arm's reach to hook the bird feeder rope onto the pole. I was so excited with the new invention, I almost didn't notice that David had put a toilet in my flower garden.

"I was just kidding when I wrote in my last column about the toilet in the garden," I said to Hubby.

"I know, but it was a good idea," David replied.

"No, it's not; you need to remove it," I said, my voice sounding edgy.

David started to laugh and then mentioned he was off to find his beer can wind chime.

I yelled at him, "If you put that wind chime up I'm going to use your fishing rods as ground stakes in my flower garden!"

Day Two: David brings home strawberry plants. Yum! I look forward to fresh strawberry jam and pie.

I asked Hubby where he planned to plant them.

"I might just put them in the toilet that's sitting in your flower garden," he said.

59

Visions of fresh strawberry anything quickly evaporated from my brain. I told David that if he planted any fruit or vegetable in the toilet I was going to ask the company he works to send him for a load somewhere far south of Minnesota, like Mexico.

Day Three: My sweetheart designed and built an awesome new gate latch for the horse pasture. He finished it right before I was leaving for work.

"Wow!" I said, "This works really nice." I took my hand off the latch and discovered oil dripping from it.

"Sorry," David mumbled, "I should have oiled it after you tried it out, just wipe your hand on my overalls."

"That's okay, I'll run inside and wash them," I said, noticing his overalls were full of black grease.

Day Four: Hubby spends quality time playing ball with our dog and breaks one of my ceramic yard ornaments. My luck will be that I come home and find a broken unidentifiable object in its place. Please David, just buy some super glue and fix my yard ornament.

Day Five: Three more days until my love goes back on the road. I'm already making plans for the toilet in my garden.

Tractor fire may be good excuse for not fencing
June 18, 2009

It is an extremely rare occasion when I second guess our decision to move back to the country; this last Sunday was one of those times.

The weather was perfect and I was pleased my hubby David and I were making such good progress on our fencing project.

Then it happened, an unexpected event that made me want to exchange my farmer's overalls and fields for high heels and a mall.

As I was driving our tractor across the field to deliver more fence posts to the designated site, bright orange flames suddenly appeared in front of the windshield. Complete shock cornered my senses; the tractor had given me no warning at all that it was going to try to turn me into a s'more.

Fortunately, I had enough sense to stop the tractor, turn off the key and leap from the cab like a starving flea circus onto a dog.

I yelled to David who was on the opposite side of the field, "The tractor's on fire!"

He yelled back, "I can see that!"

As my rescuer walked quickly to a building where we keep a fire extinguisher, I yelled again to him, "Is it going to explode?"

David's response, "I guess it could."

"Great," I mumbled to myself, "he's a guy; he's supposed know for sure." As I waited for my beloved to come to my rescue, I watched the fire turn our tractor hood from blue to black.

I considered reaching inside the cab to retrieve my 16-ounce water bottle, but decided that the nine ounces actually left in the bottle wouldn't do much good on the 12-inch flames spread across the tractor hood. Besides, it would be my luck that

I'd catch my shirt on a shift knob or something, panic and then end up ripping off my favorite tee shirt. Nobody needed to see that site, especially the neighbors.

David interrupted my ludicrous thoughts by arriving with the fire extinguisher and dousing the flames which by this time had mellowed to only four inches high.

"What happened?" he asked.

"I don't know, I was just driving across the field and poof, flames appeared," I responded, "I wasn't even going fast."

Hubby knew this statement to be true, as I am not fond of riding inside vehicles that have no shocks. David asked to use one of my pink work gloves so he could take the fuel cap off the tractor to check inside.

"Are you nuts?" I exclaimed, "It could still explode and then you'd lose your face and hair or at the very least, your eyebrows!"

My beloved just shook his head at me and asked if I would go back to the house to call his dad so he could help tow the tractor up by the shop.

"I can help you do that," I offered.

David kissed me on the forehead and said, "That's okay Honey, you finish pounding the fence posts in the ground, Dad and I will take care of the tractor."

Hmmm.

I wasn't sure if my husband was truly concerned about me, or this fire incident turned out to be his ticket to not help put up the fence. I'd like to believe it's the first option, but the grin on David's face as he "checked" over the tractor told me a different story.

Self starting boat not just a figment
of the imagination

July 16, 2009

It was family reunion time a couple of weeks ago. Thirty-one people from five different states, three dogs, five campers, one tent and a partridge in a pear tree.

For most of the relatives, water sports rate highest on the list of fun entertainment; not so much for me. I'm a dry land person, prefer to dump the dirt out of my sandals rather than slap the side of my head to get water out of my ears.

One of my cousins tried to talk me into riding on a rubber raft behind my dad's "big boat."

"I don't know, it looks pretty scary being pulled across the water at 40 mph," I said to her, "if I wipe out, I'll die and I haven't made my will out yet."

"The boat doesn't go that fast, only 25 mph," she replied, "besides, if you die your hubby gets it all anyway."

"That's what I'm afraid of."

"Come on, give it a try," she coaxed.

"Okay, tomorrow," I said.

Tomorrow came and my sister and I were hanging out on the dock, talking about the relatives, and letting the sunfish nibble on our toes as we cooled them in the lake. The "big boat" was tied nearby.

All of a sudden, the boat engine tried to turn over by itself! My sister and I looked at each other then agreed the noise must have been something else. A few moments later, the engine turned over again and again and again.

By now, I'm freaked. No way am I going to ride behind a boat that has a mind of its own. I could just visualize my body; laying on the raft being whipped from side to side, wiping out fellow boaters and the lake's loon population.

My sister and I walked back to the house where the men were sitting around, loading the black powder muzzle and working on reducing the beer population.

"The boat engine turned over all by itself," we told the guys.

We were given a quizzical look during the brief moment of silence from the men. Then they burst out laughing and asked us what we were drinking.

"Water," I answered.

"Lake water?" my husband David asked.

"No. The boat really did try to start on its own," I replied in an I-hate-you-right-this-second tone of voice.

The men walked down to the dock, found the boat rocking gently in the water with no signs of disturbance and went back to the house to finish.

I decided to wait one more day before taking a ride behind the "big boat." There were some important things I needed to do first, like tell my children to take good care of my animals and be good people once their mother was gone.

The next day, a mess of the older children came racing up to the house from the dock and told the male population that the boat had started by itself and was still running.

"Ha! I told you so!" I said to my spouse, "you owe me an apology."

"For what?" David asked.

"For acting like I was crazy yesterday."

"But you always act crazy, how am I supposed to tell the difference?"

I ignored my man because I didn't have time to hurt him and then drive him all the way to hospital and back. Instead, I walked down to the boat and watched the men as looks of puzzlement spread across their faces.

The most experienced mechanic in the family eventually determined there was a short somewhere in the wiring between the starter and the engine. It took a trip to the store for parts and the better part of a day to fix it, but the "big boat" was finally as good as new.

Later that day, I took my ride on the rubber raft behind the big boat. It was not nearly as scary as I thought and I was so grateful I didn't lose my swimsuit or my sanity.

Toilet doubles as sink
August 13, 2009

Most family reunions have numerous events that are just too funny not to share with others. How can you not chuckle at the cousin whose homemade fireworks exploded in his suitcase? Or the relative's unsuspecting girlfriend who was asked to "tidy up" around the snort pole?

One of the incidents at my recent family reunion needs to be repeated; even though I've been threatened by relatives that at all future reunions, I'll be the one sharing a tent with all the kids under the age of eight and any other creatures that slide in under the tent flap.

The event involved a toilet, a wash basin and a family member unprepared for my father's sense of humor.

It all started when my dad decided there needed to be another commode on his premises to handle all the excess "baggage" that a large group of people would be bringing to the reunion.

Fortunately, his pole barn had its own septic system and the chore of installing a toilet was only as difficult as removing super glue from the webbed toes of a frog. Once the toilet had been secured to the cement floor in the corner of the pole barn, my father and accomplices decided a few more details were needed to complete the project.

First on the list was the need for privacy for whoever used the new "outhouse." Rope was strung through the grommets of a bright blue tarp and strung from the pole barn rafters. A homemade sign was then crafted with the word "toilet" written in six different languages and fastened near the entrance. Only a few more necessary items remained to make the bathroom complete; toilet paper, soap, water and a towel.

My dad found a small old metal basin and water pitcher and placed them near the commode. About this time, a relative appeared and was observing my dad's choice of sanitation methods.

"What are the basin and pitcher for?" the family member inquired.

"For washing your hands after using the toilet," my father replied.

"Where do you get the water from for the pitcher?" the female relative asked.

With a straight face my dad said, "From the commode, just dip the pitcher in the toilet bowl and pour it into the basin."

The expression my relative gave my father resembled that of a person who was witnessing the skin falling off another person.

"Well," she responded with the same dry humor, "you could save a step and wash your hands while you flush."

My dad laughed and said, "I suppose you could."

Wish I could say there was some bizarre experiment that took place after the conversation; but there wasn't. They just headed off to join the others to make homemade ice cream.

Oompa pa pa pa pa
September 3, 2009

I love craft fairs; especially when I can set up a booth and make a few pennies.

A couple of weeks ago, my hubby David and I drove north for a huge arts festival. Our 190,000+ mile car's trunk was filled with books, photos, note cards and all the supplies needed to sell those items. It also had necessities for a two night stay for two people (and we all know I am NOT a light packer). In the back seat was our 89 pound dog, camera equipment, a laptop computer and large framed photo.

The day of the festival, my mom and I were setting up my table when an older gentleman walked over to us and asked if we like old time music.

"Of course!" we chimed in.

"Good," he said, "Because I'll be right next to your table playing my accordion; and if I see people next to your table, I'll tone it down."

Well, he didn't "tone it down" when possible customers tried to talk to me; and by the time he had played "Turkey in the Straw" for the eighth time, I was ready to lay an egg.

Fortunately, he only played for two of the six craft day hours.

Towards the end of the day, David showed up with a huge grin on his face. "Oh, oh," I thought, "it's not good when he looks that happy."

David said, "Your dad and I went to some garage sales today."

Alarms went off in my head trying to visualize what my other half bought. Parts for something we don't own? A piece of machinery needing parts? More cats?

"I bought a garden tiller for ten bucks!" David said gleefully, "It works and even came with parts. It's just what I've been looking for."

67

I was genuinely happy for my husband; he did need a tiller, but I had one big concern; how to get it home.

"How are you going to get it home Honey? Our car was full when we drove here."

"Have you bought anything here today?"

"Yes," I said defensively, "a book and some jewelry."

I could see David thinking about what could get left behind so he could bring his tiller home.

"Don't worry about it Dear," my hubby cooed, "I'll get it all in the car."

After the craft fair, we went to my parents' place to spend the night. David was like a little kid with new toys as he showed me the other "treasures" he had bought.

"More jars?" I asked a little dismayed.

"For canning this fall," Hubby responded.

"But you already have lots of jars," I said.

"Not this size."

"Your garden isn't even going to produce enough to can this year."

"It doesn't matter, I can always buy what I need, "Hubby said.

The following day when it was time to leave, David packed the trunk with the tiller, boxes of jars and the other items we had brought up. The dog had a little less space in the back seat and I had the camera bag and computer on my lap.

When we made a stop for gas, my beloved casually commented that we were riding a little low. Go figure. Ten minutes later, down the road, he was lamenting because I refused to let him stop at a garage sale.

Next trip we take I'm renting a U-Haul.

Hubby puts on his cleanest dirty shirt
September 17, 2009

Going to church on Sunday morning with my husband David is a lot like taking a toddler to, well, church on Sunday morning.

I pick out my spouse's clothes. After all, it's hard to choose a pair of pants and shirt that you know you are not allowed to wear while changing the oil in my car, right?

So, after my beloved is spit shined and polished, he heads to the kitchen for beer bread. Yes, beer bread; but not to eat a slice before we leave for the church; no, it is what David baked to bring for the social time after the service.

"I appreciate you making something for this morning Honey," I said, "I ran out of time between work, a wedding reception and other commitments."

"No problem, my love muffin," Hubby responds.

"I do have one question for you though; why beer bread, why not banana or zucchini bread?"

"Well, sometimes the little plastic communion cup isn't as full of wine as I think it should be, so this is a way to top it off."

Hmmmm, I think to myself, just how much beer did Hubby put in the batter anyway?

Sitting in the pew before the service started, David asks, "Do I smell like skunk?"

I lean in a little closer to him and sniff, "No," I whisper, "your cologne covers it up."

The reason David would ask me this is because the night before, our dog Isaiah got up close and personal with a skunk. It was a mad dash to the car Sunday morning trying to outrun Isaiah so he wouldn't get near us with his own "wild kingdom" perfume scent.

69

The service starts and as usual, my spouse is paging through the hymnal looking for pictures. It's not that he doesn't have a sincere faith or dislikes church; David just has the attention span of a snowman in June. And as much as his mother loves him, she refuses to sit next to him in church.

When it's time for the children's sermon in front of church, my sweetheart looks at me with sad eyes. He has been warned several times to not even ask if he can join the five year olds during this time. I have learned to carry lemon drops in my purse to give my 44 year old husband as a reward for not whining during this ten-minute service segment.

I manage to enjoy my time in God's house even with David digging in my purse for crayons, poking me in the ribs just for the fun of it or trying to make me laugh while he plays "Here's the church, here's the steeple..." with his hands.

After the service, my other half sits calmly at a table with other adults, drinks coffee and eats donuts without a trail of crumbs down his shirt. He is a kind, mature man talking about the weather, the economy and how he looks forward to next Sunday. I, on the other hand, am asking young mothers who they recommend for a baby-sitter.

It's hard to find a parking spot too close
October 8, 2009

Hubby thinks I pick on him too much; making fun of his every little quirk. I disagree; my beloved David just needs a tad of redirection concerning certain areas of his life; like parking.

It's usually the women who get made fun of in the area of driving, not in our household. David likes to park close; which in its self is not a bad thing if the space is already available. But making laps for "just one space closer to the store door" gets old after awhile.

I tell my spouse, "Let's walk, it's good for us and we need it."

He replies, "Parking close means we don't have to carry what we bought so far."

I say, "That's what carts are for."

And then he answers back, "After you push the cart to the car, you have to push it back to the store and that's extra walking."

I drop the subject and resolve to the fact that David is a "close space" guy.

Interestingly enough, when we went to the State Fair this year, David drove to one of the farther corners of the parking lot where we planned to leave our vehicle then ride a bus to the fairgrounds.

After several laps around the lot, my other half parked beneath a small tree; first pulling up next to it so my door was close to it; then turning the car around so his side was closest to the tree.

"What are you doing?" I asked David.

"Parking in the shade," he replied.

"But there are no leaves on the tree," I said.

"So, the branches will still help keep the car cool."

I looked at my husband with disbelief. "You do know that by the time we get back to the car tonight, that it will be dark and the "shade" tree won't make a difference?" I remarked.

David thought about my comment a moment, started the car back up and drove around the parking lot a few more laps before finally settling on a space close to where the bus would pick us up.

There doesn't seem to be an issue of parking at our house; David parks whatever, wherever he happens to be.

This is in reference more to objects in the house than outside. It's amazing how quickly my hubby's male brain forgets where an item originated from. I'm really not a "neat freak;" it's just that I don't understand why pajama bottoms can't go back in the drawer and tools can't go back in the tool box. Is there something comforting about pretending to not know where clean dishes get put away or feigning ignorance that greasy sweatshirts don't belong on the back of the couch? Does my beloved enjoy teasing me by saying he'll put his stuff away, only to still have it sitting in the same spot two weeks later?

I'm trying to learn to relax a little bit about "everything in its place"; but please David, don't you think leaving sheet rock dust on the kitchen counters is a bit much?

Husband sold in horse trade at craft fair
November 12, 2009

Tis the season for craft fairs; and my supportive hubby David, is right there with me.

At the most recent fair where I had a booth, he was a fantastic help. My beloved helped with the loading, hauling and setting up my wares. He even made an extra trip home for more products. There are however, a few minor suggestions I have for him for the next craft fair.

My spouse thinks that every time a potential customer walks by my booth, I should run out like a circus barker and give a lengthy sales pitch. I tried to explain to David that if someone is interested in what I have for sale, I will be more than happy at that time to talk to them.

That answer is not good enough for David, so he takes it upon himself to talk to EVERYBODY who comes within 15 feet of my booth. Sometimes the topic of conversation strays from what I have available for sale to my hubby trying to give away my horses.

I tell the person David is talking to that," If you take my horse, my husband goes with it."

That comment quickly puts an end to anyone wanting my horses.

Fortunately, people at craft fairs have a sense of humor which leads to them treating my husband like he's part of an entertainment act.

Another slightly annoying habit Hubby has is standing in front of my booth so people can't see what I have available. My sweetheart is not exactly the size and shape of a pencil. Although I love him as he is, it is just not possible for people to see through him. I had to continually tell him to go sit in the chair in the corner of the booth and behave himself.

Finally, I've had to tell David not to say to me, "You don't need to buy that, you can make it yourself at home."

"Right," I respond. "Just as soon as I don't work two jobs, buy a woodshop, supplies and tools for making candles, stained glass, pottery and soap."

My spouse then expresses how fun it might be to make items in his workshop for craft fairs.

I tell him "Just as soon as you take care of the unfinished projects in my kitchen first. You know, like taping and texturing the wall you messed up last summer or replacing the false front drawer with a real one."

David gives me a deflated look, so I try to lift his spirits by saying, "Think of the things you need to do at home as practice for the things you want to do in your workshop. By the time you finish in the house, your crafts will be of the highest quality. Oh, and one more thing Sweetie, will you please build me a display wall before the next craft fair?"

I'm not sure Hubby really believed what I was saying, but because he's such a great guy, he just smiles and says, "Yes, my love muffin."

Easy to find reasons to be thankful
November 26, 2009

It is turkey time at the Riedeman house. Well, not exactly real turkey. Unfortunately, my sweet hubby David and poultry do not get along, so I take an alternative and try to sculpt it into something that resembles something traditional.

Have you ever tried to carve a ham into the shape of a turkey? Its not easy, one wrong cut, and bang, all of a sudden you're left with a hunk of meat that looks like a chewed up dog toy. With the proper glaze the ham can come close to the color and texture of a finely cooked turkey. Add a large handful of garnish and ta da, the imitation bird sits on the table.

You can't have turkey without stuffing, it is just un-American. Since stuffing does not top the list of items David prefers to eat, I make a dish that looks like stuffing but is not. I won't tell you what the ingredients are, just be confident that the food items include brown lumps and a few spices.

As for myself, I really don't care for cranberries, so my beloved replaces my potion with purple grapes soaked in grape juice tinted with a bit of red food coloring. It's pretty close to the real thing. I also don't care for sweet potatoes or yams which means finding another option to re-create. Pumpkin guts mixed with brown sugar? No, don't like pumpkin guts either unless baked in a pie.

Speaking of pies, both David and I like pumpkin pie. He also adores pecan and peanut butter (not mixed together of course). I prefer chocolate and blackberry (also not mixed together). The dessert category is one area we don't need to worry about.

Food replacements have got me thinking of other kinds of replacements; no, not my hubby, he is just too adorable and fun. I was referring to substituting the negative with positive. Finding the plus side to mashed potatoes on the kitchen walls and whipped cream on the carpet.

Laughing at a washing machine and dishwasher that both break on a day where every dish and towel gets dirty. Choose to make fun of myself instead of other people. Using humor as a way to ease the stress of a busy time of the year and bring a smile to the face of others.

I want to make sure I tell God this week and always, "thanks for giving me your love, a family, friends, a home, jobs and animals to round out the jagged corners of life."

I hope this week you can rejoice even when your least favorite person decides to visit and the kids feed the dog things that make him throw up on your lap. In the chaos of designing the "perfect" holiday, I pray the most precious moments are the ones you and others will recall with the words, "I remember Thanksgiving of 2009...."

Education provided by 50 years of experience
December 10, 2009

It was a major milestone for me last week; I turned 50. Yes 50; the big 5-0, the half century mark, the black balloons and "make fun of the old lady" jokes.

I am older than my husband, older than my sisters and obviously, older than my kids so I know more than the people who like to tease me. (What I actually know isn't relevant.)

Here is a list of the things I've learned over the last five decades:

Laughter is so good for the soul that I make fun of my husband every chance I get. (But don't think the man doesn't return the favor, just check out his laugh lines.)

Don't bring your male dog to the Christmas tree farm to help pick out a tree. You will be buying a lot of Christmas trees because he marked all the ones that he liked; which is pretty much most of them.

Following a recipe exactly does not guarantee it will still be edible. Most likely the day you try it the garbage disposal will not work, you will have unexpected company and the leftovers will make the dog and cat puke.

What is guaranteed is the fact you will never be "carded" at the liquor store again unless it pertains to your AARP card.

It will snow the one night of the week you do not put your car in the garage, you can only find one mitten and forgot to order propane for the furnace.

Don't accept any "free" animal unless the giver is also paying for a pet accident insurance policy.

Husbands seem to lose their understanding of the English language when you tell them, "Honey, could you please have such and such fixed in the next two weeks." They seem to interpret the phrase as, "Okay, I'll have it done in the first two weeks of 2012."

No matter how much you prepare for a special event, you will always forget something.

Your children will forget your birthday, but remember the two dollars you borrowed from them eight years ago.

I have become a citizen in the world of large print, books on tape and chains for my glasses.

The man who will do anything for you, is still not able to coordinate his own set of clothing for any occasion without your help.

I did not know until the day I turned 50 that the body can produce bumps, age spots, moles, excessive hair and saggy everything in a matter of hours.

There are two sides to the argument of eating healthy and exercising regularly. Side one supports eating right and strengthening the muscles so you can live longer. The other side says enjoy the wine, chocolate and the occasional evening in front of the T.V. because you don't know how long you will live. I opt for a compromise between the two theories, eating a chocolate bar while walking the dog.

At the end of the day, loving God, your family and friends is what really counts.

Sack of horse feed high on Christmas wish list
December 31, 2009

It is a fascinating process in which my beloved husband David tries to decide on what to buy me for birthdays, anniversaries and Christmas.

First of all, he knows gifts are not necessary to start with. A card is more than enough sentiment for me. Second of all, if he wants to purchase an item, it does not have to be expensive. I'm happy with chocolate covered cherries or a warm pair of socks.

Here is how the conversation goes when it comes time to celebrate a special occasion.

"What do you want for your (birthday, anniversary or Christmas?)" David asks.

"I don't know; you don't have to get me anything," I reply.

"Yes, I do. It's mandatory as a husband."

"Okay, how about a music CD or sack of horse feed."

"Those are not very good choices," Hubby says, "It should be something more than $20."

"Well, how about an iPod or external hard drive for my computer."

"Would you really use either one of those?"

"Yes."

"Those things are a lot of money."

"Well then, how about tickets to a play?"

"I don't know which play you would like. Besides, you work all the time."

"No, I don't. And you know what kind of plays I like."

"You are so hard to buy for," David says with exasperation in his voice.

"Don't buy me anything then, just do dishes for a month."

My spouse's eyes widen to the size of baseballs, he turns pale and looks like he is about to pass out.

79

"What?" I ask, "That won't cost you anything but time."

"That is an unreasonable gift suggestion," said David.

"What is a reasonable gift then?"

"I don't know, but not that."

"Why don't you wander around in Fleet Farm; I'm sure you'll find something there, especially in the horse section."

"You don't need any more horse stuff."

At this point in the conversation, we are both frustrated. David thinks I'm unreasonable to buy for and I think I'm easy to buy for.

When the day finally arrives for my gift, I am presented with a card that says, "I owe you a nice dinner and movie."

I am genuinely grateful and look forward to the evening when the two of us have the opportunity to enjoy the present together. Of course, with the schedules we both have, my underwear drawer is full of "I owe yous."

The day will come though, when we will have the opportunity to sit in the movie theatre for hours on end and travel from restaurant to restaurant sampling delicious meals. Till then, I'll continue to strain my brain in trying to think of gift ideas that my beloved can buy that neither break the bank or makes him feel cheap.

2010

When you laugh at yourself, world laughs
January 14, 2010

Winter can be a beautiful time of year, pure white fields of snow, icicles that sparkle in the sunlight. Sometimes that loveliness though, can be the cause of events frustrating enough to make a person dip themselves in chocolate and eat their own hand off.

I have a friend who shared an incident that happened to her during one of the more uncomfortable days of winter.

Marian was sitting in her vehicle when she decided to put her hat on before exiting her car. She leaned forward, put her hat on and when she straightened up, her knuckles accidentally hit the sunroof button of her vehicle. The sunroof opened and Marian was baptized in a heavy load of snow. Her purse was sitting on the seat next to her and it also was filled to the top with the wet winter wonder.

A group of us laughed along with Marian as she told us about the event, she said, "Wait, there's more to the story."

I tried to visualize what could have happened next. I figured the heater in the car was on high turning the snow instantly into water and then when Marian stepped out of the vehicle, the cold temperature encased her in a shell of ice. What did happen to my friend was not too far off from my imagination.

The day after the sunroof fiasco, Marian decided to take her vehicle through the carwash. Unknown to her, when she closed the sunroof the day before, it did not close all the way because of snow left in the rails. This meant that my friend was surprised for the second day in a row by liquid coming from her sunroof. Her carefully applied make-up slid down her face like bacon grease slides off a china plate.

When Marian had finished going through the carwash, a man came up to her and said, "Did you know your sunroof was open?"

My friend didn't tell us what she said to him, but I'm pretty sure it's not printable.

When we got home from our visit with Marian and our other friends, my husband David said to me, "If what happened to Marian happened to me, I'm not sure I would tell anyone."

"I would," I replied.

"You would tell others if it happened to you?" Hubby asked.

"Yes, and I would tell others if it happened to you," I said.

"Don't you think it's kind of an embarrassing story?"
"No, it's in the same category of things that occurs every day to people. Like when you put corn syrup instead of vegetable oil in the deep fryer."

"That was not funny, that was an accident," my spouse says defensively.

"Exactly, it was a harmless accident that was funny. We need to laugh at ourselves Honey. As they say, "the world needs more humor."

"You laugh everyday at me," David says in a voice searching for sympathy.

"Not *every day*."

"When have you not?" Hubby asks.

"Okay, maybe I do; but that's because you are so cute."

"I'm not cute, I'm macho."

"Okay, whatever, will you please take the garbage out?"

"Yes, my love muffin."

No spinning donuts on Sundays
January 28, 2010

Sundays are the designated "weird" days at the Riedeman household.

It is usually Sundays when accidents occur, items get lost and something happens to one or more of our animals.

Let's start with accidents. Although the following incident is not a true "accident" it's still within a subtitle of the meaning.

Its common knowledge my hubby David likes to spin donuts on the ice. Since he's not allowed to do so on roads or in heavily populated parking lots, he chose this last Sunday to do in our driveway, with my car. And you guessed it; he managed to get stuck in the only snow bank by our house, which is way beyond our plowed drive.

I would have laughed harder than I did except I was in the car with David and I was concerned he might think I was making fun of him and leave my vehicle buried in the snow until spring.

The real comedy arrived later though after several attempts to free my car from the bank's icy grip. Hubby tried shoveling the snow around the car, sticking a chain under the tire and pushing it back and forth while I was kept putting the car in forward and reverse. (That almost caused another accident when he was behind the vehicle pushing forward while I had it in reverse pushing on the gas).

My spouse wondered why the vehicle was so hard to pull out. To his surprise, he discovered he had left the emergency brake on. Which I didn't understand since the car was clearly not going anywhere.

When my car was safely in the garage, David decided to fix the cigarette lighter in it so I could plug in the charger for my cell phone. After some undetermined amount of time, I was informed "not to touch anything close to that area."

I gave my beloved a quizzical look and asked, "Does my radio and cassette player still work?"

"I think so," he replied. "I'll fix it next weekend, I need a special tool."

I didn't say anything and went into the house to look for something we lost even though I'm not sure what it is.

As expected, the animals didn't fail this last Sunday either in creating a near crisis.

During the football game halftime, Hubby went outside to get more firewood. He promptly came back in and yelled for my help.

"What's wrong," I said in a voice filled with panic.

"It's your cat, he's meowing and I can't find him."

"Which cat?"

"Snot. Grab a flashlight and let's see if we can find him."

Both of us were dressed in snow boots, coats and pajamas; fumbling around in the wet snow calling, "here kitty, kitty."

We finally found the distressed feline locked in the outhouse behind our garage.

"How the heck did he get in there?" I asked.

David walked around the small building and discovered a section of mesh pulled back from the vent. He examined the hole in the outhouse and said that the cat had managed to come up through that hole.

I had been holding Snot and after David's observation, quickly put him down to walk on his own.

The rest of the day was pretty uneventful except for a spilled bowl of popcorn and exploding can of pop.

Skiing relationship all downhill
February 11, 2010

A long, long time ago when I was a giddy and naïve teenager, I had a boyfriend who decided to teach me to ski. He outfitted me in the trendiest ski garb of the time; lime green snow pants and jacket, lime green ski hat, bright yellow ski boots and goggles large enough to double as an astronaut helmet.

I think the purpose of the goggles though was so I wouldn't blind myself when I looked in the mirror. Anyway, I thought I looked like a professional snow bunny. I worried a bit though; about the set of skis and poles that lay before me like two sets of giant chopsticks I knew I would never be able to coordinate.

Once on the slopes the boyfriend asked me, "Are you excited?"

"Yeah, but scared, "I replied with chattering teeth.

"There's nothing to it."

"Easy for you to say, you've been doing it for years."

"Don't worry; a couple of runs down the bunny hill and you'll be an expert."

Such words of comfort from the boy who attempted back flips off an icy slope and ended up in the hospital in traction.

After a dozen runs down the bunny slope, my legs were shaking and I was still unable to keep my ski tips uncrossed. My skis were so far apart that small children were using me as a human tunnel.

Apparently the boyfriend had more confidence in me than I had in myself, because I belatedly noticed that the next ski lift we were on went to an expert run, not the bunny hill.

"Wait a minute, where are we going?!" I shrieked.

"You're past beginner, you're an intermediate skier now," he boasted to himself.

"No, I'm not!"

"Yes you are. Besides, you won't get better unless you challenge yourself."

"This is not considered 'challenging oneself' this is your subtle way of committing murder. Why don't you just tell me that you don't want to date me anymore?"

The boyfriend just laughed as I told him in the most controlled angry voice I could muster, "This is Devil's Run. I'm not going down this run, it has bumps on it."

"They're called moguls."

"I don't do moguls."

"Watch me, they're not that hard. Ski to the top of a mogul, turn, then ski down between the valleys of moguls and back to the top of another one."

I hung onto my ski poles as if they were the anticipated crutches I was sure I would end up on. I leaned forward and pushed off. I missed the turns through the miniature mogul valleys and continued over the top of the moguls; my head bouncing like a ski bunny bobble head. My stomach sprung to the top of my throat like a small child on a trampoline. I no longer had control of my legs as I had left them back at the ski lodge some time ago. My pain finally ended when I hit a soft mogul head-on and got my skis stuck.

Obviously the boyfriend and I didn't stay together as a couple; but he did teach me a valuable lesson: Dressing like a snow bunny, doesn't make you ski like one.

Even borrowed flowers are better than no flowers
February 25, 2010

Valentine's Days – hearts, candy, flowers and the one holiday Hubby had better not mess up.

I gave my husband David, his Valentine's Day presents the night of February 13 because we were going out of town on the 14th. My gifts to him were a special picture frame with a photo of us, a box of candy and a card full of mushy sentiments.

David gave me a look of panic. "I thought we were going out to eat tomorrow?"

"We are," I said.

"Well, I didn't buy you a present."

"Yes you did, you got me that box of chocolates from the truck stop last week."

Hubby then got a determined look on his face before disappearing for a few minutes. When he came back into the bathroom where I was brushing my teeth, he set a container of red tulips and an envelope on the counter.

"Here are some flowers for you," my beloved said with pride.

"I bought those tulips to bring to my mother tomorrow," I replied.

"Well here, I'm giving them to you."

"I bought them for my mother."

"I didn't buy you flowers because I thought we were done with that flower thing."

"That flower thing? What does that mean?"

"We've been married long enough and I –"

Don't finish your sentence or I'll have to hurt you."

I concentrated on opening the envelope of the card my beloved gave me. A dozen M&Ms fell out all over the counter and floor.

"Are these the M&Ms from the candy jar on the kitchen counter?'

"Maybe."

The card was cute; a dog with a lipstick kiss on its forehead and the words "I can be real bad" on the inside of the card.

Bad? He's already in trouble most of the time.

So, as we're driving through Brainerd, David whips through a parking lot and stops in front of small stand of flowers. He surveys his choices. "$25 for a dozen roses or $15 for a bunch of carnations," he reads off the sign. "I don't like your mom that much; matter of fact, I don't like you that much," David says in a teasing tone of voice.

"Funny Honey."

During a conversation with my parents about Valentine's Day, my mom talked about her own holiday story.

It seems that my dad insisted she buy a red bra during their latest trip to Wal-Mart. Mom was not too enthused about the idea, so she put the bra in dad's shopping cart.

When they got home she tried it on, commenting to my dad that it didn't feel right. The tags explained why, it was a push-up bra. My mom is over sixty five and has never owned such a contraption.

According to Mom, Dad's eyes got wide and he said, "Is *THAT* how those things fit?"

"I'm glad I left the tags on the bra, it goes back to the store on our next trip there," my mom said.

"Speaking of Wal-Mart, we stopped there too and I bought you something mom," said David. He left for a moment and returned with a pot of red tulips.

Fuming over false flattery, feathered friends
March 11, 2010

As much as we love each other, sometimes my husband David and I aren't able to come to a "meeting of the minds." Two future events are in the forefront of this situation. One involves his upcoming appointments with the dentist, the other concerns chickens.

My spouse told me he was buying the dental assistant who was scheduled to work on his teeth, chocolate.

"I think I'll buy her a rose too; a red one the first week and a black rose the second week," said David.

"Why are you even considering giving her candy and flowers?" I asked.

"So it doesn't hurt as bad when she works on my teeth."

"You can't bribe her to not do what she has to do," I replied as I rolled my eyes, "and explain to me the red rose and black rose theory."

"Actually, the black rose is only if I'm really in a lot of pain after the first week."

I was silent for a moment before I asked, not too sweetly either; "How come she gets flowers and candy and I didn't get any from you for Valentine's Day?"

"You did get stuff from me."

"Don't even try to excuse what you did for Valentine's Day."

Hubby knew not to "debate" the issue any further, so he changed the subject.

Sure enough though, when I got home from work the next day, my husband had bought a chocolate Easter bunny for his dental assistant. I hope the dentist forgets the Novocain.

As for the chicken issue; David knows chickens are one of the last two legged creatures I want living on our property. We've had many discussions about my dislike for those clucking feather dusters.

"I don't understand why you don't want chickens." my spouse says.

"I don't understand why you do; you don't eat any form of poultry, it takes us three weeks to go through a dozen eggs and the smell of chicken poop ranks right up there with skunk smell," I said firmly.

"You're exaggerating," David remarks.

"Am I? Do you eat chicken?"

"Well no, but –"

"Do you eat eggs every day?"

"How can I, I'm not here every day."

"Exactly, that's my point; we don't need chickens," I said on the verge of extreme anger.

So what does David decide to do? Prints out chicken coop designs from the Internet and orders chickens from the local feed store. He tries to endear me to the poultry program by describing the color of the birds to me. Apparently, three hens and one rooster are due to arrive sometime in May. I have decided to ignore the situation for now; there are still a couple of months to "hatch" my own plan to get rid of the chickens, or maybe I'll add a bunk bed to the coop for David to sleep in.

Spring clean up results in close shave
March 25, 2010

I think spring should be associated with more than the promise of new growth and cleaning. Forgiveness is another word that comes to my mind. I am so grateful that God forgives me. And I really try to forgive others, especially my beloved husband David, who decided to experiment with his facial hair one night.

It started when Hubby said he was going to shave his neck area. He took my electric hair trimmer and went to work. A few minutes later he came into the room where I was sitting with a big smile on his face.

"What did you do to your beard?" I asked while trying not to laugh too hard at the two bushy stripes on either side of his mouth and the two triangles he tried to pass off as sideburns.

"What do you mean?"

"I mean, you cannot leave whatever that is on your face. And I'm really not trying to be mean, but you look like a walrus."

"Thanks, I love you too," replied hubby in a pouty voice. He turned around and went back into the bathroom. Five minutes later he was back with the Oliver Hardy look.

I didn't say anything, I really didn't want to hurt my hubby's feelings any more than I had. Since he's a pretty sharp guy though, he was able to figure out through my expression that an improvement had not been made.

For the third time, David went back into the bathroom. Instead of the buzz of the clippers, I hear him saying, "Oh no!"

"What's wrong?" I shouted.

"The clippers quit working!"

I walked into the bathroom just as my spouse was banging the clippers against the counter, micro sized bits of whiskers landing in every corner of the room. He couldn't get the hair clippers to work, so he tried the battery operated nose hair clippers. Those wouldn't work either. David had to settle for a hand held razor with a dull blade.

"See all the trouble I went through just for you," said my hubby as he rubbed a good smelling aftershave on his bald face.

"I never told you to cut off your entire beard."

"Well, I was tired of you saying that I carried around a whole meal in it or that it made me look old."

"I'm sorry Honey, but you frequently did have bits of food hiding in your beard and it DID make you look older than you are," I said, "besides, I only wanted you to trim it up a bit."

"I'm not going to shave off a beard anymore," David said stubbornly, "you'll just have to live with a man with a beard that goes to his belly button."

It was late, I was tired and there was whisker stubble embedded in bars of soap in my bathroom. I decided a conversation regarding beards could be discussed another time.

Some pain involved in midlife makeover
April 8, 2010

"I quit!" my devoted husband David said to me the other night.

"What are you quitting?" I asked.

"All future attempts at things that are supposed to be good for my health."

"What are you talking about?"

My hubby then launched into elaborate detail about how every time he tries to do the right thing it backfires on him. The first example had to do with his teeth. David has been getting some work done on them to get them into ship shape. As expected, the dentist and assistants remind him of the importance of brushing and flossing. Then my spouse calls me a couple days ago from Georgia and tells me he broke a tooth while flossing his teeth.

"This is what I mean about doing the right thing. I floss, break a tooth and now my tongue is all cut up from the sharp edges," David says in frustration.

The next area of personal health has to do with exercising. On Saturdays, David has been bowling with his dad. I think the sport is producing favorable results to my hubby's body. He thinks otherwise.

"Everything hurts on my body, my legs, my feet, my arms, even my eyelids hurt," the man whined.

"How can your eyelids hurt?" I ask.

"I don't know, but they do."

The last few weekends David, our dog and I have been taking walks together. During the most recent venture, the distance was slightly longer than the first two times (a little over an hour). Once we get home, David informs me that the walk just about killed him.

"Honey," I say to my beloved, "the walk was on a paved path without any inclines higher than four inches. How can you possibly hurt that bad?"

"Just look at the dog, he's dying too," David says.

I look at the dog and he looks back at me, no obvious signs of discomfort that I can tell.

The final issue of discontentment in David's personal "health department" has to do with food. He has informed me that eating "rabbit food" all day is not helping him lose weight.

"All it does is make me want to hop to the bathroom and scratch my nose," David says with a huge sigh.

I look at my spouse and see changes in him that he doesn't. They are good things and I respect his frustration at the difficult process to get there.

"You know what Honey, just have more patience, soon you'll see what I see," I tell him sweetly.

"Well, I'd better start seeing results soon or I'm going back to eating deep friend pickles and watching NASCAR from a prone position on the couch."

I just shake my head and leave the room. If I give him anymore encouragement he'll probably go back to doing a few more of his old habits. I am not ready to retrain him to not

Nine lives plus sixth sense equals animal crackers
April 22, 2010

There are some days I feel my beloved pets are smarter than me.

How do they know when I'm on the phone or in the shower? How do the cats know that if they take out the entire contents of my purse they will find an atom size piece of candy wrapped in plastic and buried beneath four dollars of change?

How does my dog Isaiah know when I'm merely resting or in a deep sleep? He seems to have figured out to bark at nothing right in the middle of my REM cycle. (I blame my hubby David; I tell him that the dog thinks his snoring is actually wild bears fighting in our bedroom.)

As for the horses, they are normally content to play fight with each other or chase after any cat that wanders into their pasture.

Last week though, I was bombarded with predicaments from the dog, cats and horses. It started with my Isaiah. He owns what is referred to as a "Jolly" ball. A large heavy duty ball designed to take the tough teeth of horses and large dogs. It has a handle and is similar to a Hippity Hop.

As I was slowly and carefully backing out of my driveway, Isaiah decided to drop the ball so it rolled perfectly under my car while it was in motion. Since the ball isn't designed to pop, it wedged tight under my car causing it my car to high center. It took a moment to figure out why the car backed up with difficulty and the dog was barking furiously at the vehicle. I tried using a broom to get the ball out, but it was hopelessly stuck. So out came the 45-ton floor jack that takes a mule to pull around. I managed to get it under my car, jack it up and then extract the Jolly ball. I told my dog, "Don't ever do that again or I'm going to take your toy away." Isaiah just looked at me with his big, brown trusting eyes and his tongue hanging out. What's a girl to do?

I am blessed with four horses that usually reserve their curiosity for grain buckets and candy cane treats. On the same day the dog decided to "drop the ball," one of the horses decided to experiment with the gate latch.

Boredom must have reached an all time high for the equines, because the next thing I know I'm receiving a phone call that they were out on the road. I guess they decided it was time for a field trip to town. (Thank you and God bless you my wonderful neighbors who stopped and put them in.) Fortunately, there was no incident to any property or humans. There was a little damage to our yard. Our recently reseeded and vacuumed lawn (by David the day before) has a few horse hoof prints and the horses' own brand of fertilizer.

Apparently the cats didn't want to be left out on this particular day of mayhem, so one of them without a previous history of getting into trouble, decided to try a pull up on a curtain rod. I can just envision the other three cats cheering on the newest addition to our home. "Come on Joe, you can do it!" Joe a seven pound "kitten" brought down the rod and curtains. Scattering the pegs to a large cribbage board nearby and taking pictures off the wall.

The difference I discovered between scolding my sweet animals and scolding my sweet husband when he gets in trouble is this: My pets usually don't repeat the same naughty behavior.

Entertained by tales of the road
May 10, 2010

There are many things I love about my husband David; one of my favorites is listening to him tell "trucking" stories; those interesting tales of life of the highway as seen through a man with a huge sense of humor.

One of the most recent events revolves around a tornado. (No pun intended.)

David was driving through Huntsville, Alabama after having dropped off a load in Tennessee. The sky and weather conditions all pointed towards a nasty storm about to hit. Sure enough, as Hubby came down a hill and rounded a bend in the road, a tornado could be seen in the distance. My spouse cranked the old semi truck into a higher gear and left Huntsville at a high rate of speed. When he wasn't too far out of town, another truck driver started talking to David on the CB radio.

"Hey Buddy; you're going kinda fast there, aren't you? Where you headed to in such a hurry?"

"Look behind you Bucko!" David said, "There's a tornado headed this way."

Apparently the other truck driver looked in his mirrors because he responded on the radio with a "oh *&%$#! There is a tornado chasing us! I was wondering why traffic going into town had slowed down and come to a stop."

Duh.

It was a rock and roll ride for David and anybody else on the road for the next couple of miles, but they fortunately were able to out run the tornado.

***

A couple of days ago David called from the road and said to me, "I'm beginning to feel really loved this week."

"Really?" I replied, "Why is that?"

"Because there are so many cars passing me by that give me the one finger wave.

"I don't think that's an indication that they like you," I said.

"Well, at least I don't return the sentiment," David replied proudly.

"Do you just ignore them?"

"No, I pull up beside their vehicle, honk my horn and blow them a kiss."

I tried to visualize my big, burly husband blowing a kiss to another big, burly, *pissed off* man. I shook my head to clear that disturbing image.

"And how do they respond to that gesture?" I asked David.

"They usually get even madder than they were and either speed away from me or give me a one fingered wave with both hands."

I could see no point in telling my beloved to behave himself when in actuality he wasn't doing anything wrong. This led me to wonder why drivers gave him the one finger to start with. When I asked him about it, he guessed that the others drivers probably thought he didn't drive fast enough or passing was more difficult with a semi truck in the way. That made sense so I dropped the subject.

The next day David called and said, "I just saw the oddest thing........"

Chicken situation normal, all fowled up
June 10, 2010

It's a fowl situation at our hobby farm.

My sweet husband David waited anxiously for his four hens to arrive this month. For the last few weeks, he has been teased about getting the birds.

"You can't eat chicken David; you're allergic to it, so why do you want those stinky birds?" I asked, not really wanting to hear the answer.

"For the eggs," he responded.

"We don't eat enough eggs to justify having chickens. It takes us two or three weeks to go through a carton of eggs."

"It doesn't matter, we'll sell the eggs. Besides, I want something on our place that's mine. You have the dog, cats and horses, I want chickens," my beloved said emphatically.

"First of all," I argued, "you love all these animals as much as I do. In fact, you were the one who bought me two of the horses and you were the one who brought home two more cats." I was starting to get a little irritated at his refusal to admit how much our pets meant to him.

"I know you," my hubby said softly, "once you see those cute yellow fuzzy chicks, you'll start spoiling them just like all the other critters around here."

"I doubt I'll be kissing them on the beak anytime soon."

"Go ahead and keep giving me a bad time," David said, "each time you do, I'm going to buy another chick. I've already named three of them; Tami, Janet and Bonnie."

"You must have a death wish naming chickens after your wife, mother and mother-in-law," I retorted. "And if you insist on buying lots of chickens, you might as well plan to build a chicken coop behind the cab of your semi because that's where they'll be living."

"Why are so against having chickens?" my spouse asked. "I don't need one more thing to take care of right now."

"They will be almost maintenance free. I'm building a deluxe chicken coop, complete with linoleum flooring. There will be automatic feeders and waterers, you shouldn't have to do hardly anything," David said with confidence.

The day arrived to pick up the chickens, so I made a 30 mile special trip to get them and bring them home right away. David had already made a temporary home in the shop for these birds until they were old enough to go out into the coop. The entire time I'm driving back and forth and getting the chickens settled David is calling me, wanting to make sure his "babies" are okay.

"Take a picture with your cell phone and send it to me," Hubby says jubilantly. "I want to see my girls."

I obediently take a couple of photos and send them to him. Within a few moments, David is calling me back.

"You have the wrong chickens," he said in a panic.

"Those birds are half grown."

"Yes they are the right chickens and yes they are half grown. And in case you didn't notice, they are not cute. They have the head of a fuzzy chick and the body of a hen half plucked.

I have to go now honey, because these 'low maintenance' birds need to have the heat lamp readjusted their food and water relocated to higher ground and I need to make sure they don't get out of their containment."

One more thing my love, I renamed your hens, you can now call them Breakfast, Lunch, Dinner and Snack. Or do you prefer Chicken Cordon Bleu, Hot Wings, Chicken Nuggets and Chicken Strips?"

"That's not nice Tami, we aren't planning to eat these chickens."

"You're right, but something else might."

It's been almost a week now since David's feathered friends arrived and something strange has happened; those beady eyes and tiny chirps have gotten to me. I find myself telling Hubby about the silly antics his birds perform and I no longer visualize them as a meal on a plate. I guess that makes them officially part of the KoodB Ranch family and a part of my critter family.

Now if David starts talking about pigs....

Davids participate in tractor push event
June 24, 2010

On Father's Day my husband David and my dad (also named David) decided to do a project together. This always causes my mother to get a worried look on her face and me to double check my spouse's life insurance policy.

They pushed our 35 year old small garden tractor into the garage so a drive belt could be replaced. Apparently putting on the new belt wasn't a problem, only starting the tractor and trying to drive it creates issues.

The first thing David (my husband) told my father was stand back, "the tractor smokes a bit when I start it up. It also smokes when I drive it. Don't worry though; it doesn't smoke when it's shut off."

This would explain why my dad had a halo of black circling his head when he came into the house later that day.

"Look on the plus side," he said, "the mosquitoes are gone from the garage."

The next couple of things that happened had to do with trying to get the tractor into gear to move it into another building.

You need to know first, that a couple of years ago, my hubby took that tractor completely apart to rebuild the engine and paint the body. When he put it back together, he didn't repaint the gear pattern.

What this meant on Father's Day, is that when my husband David sat on the tractor, started it up and put it in a gear, he didn't know what gear he was putting it in. This ancient implement reared up like the Lone Ranger's horse. My dad suggested to David that he get a counter balance for the front of the tractor. "Guess I could always get another seat and steering wheel to face me and I could have Tami operate the tractor from that end."

When the guys got done chuckling over that idea, they tried another gear to see if they could get the tractor to go forward.

After it reared up again it did go forward, right into our wall of coolers, condensing them all from a full to mini size.

On the third attempt at the gear selection, the tractor reared up once more before going backwards. This would have been fine except that when the guys put gas in the tractor, they set the gas can behind it. This last maneuver put a hole in the gas can. "I wouldn't use that gas can," my dad said laughing, "It might leak." Cute, everyone's a comedian.

After a delicious BBQ, David and David talked about hooking something to that small garden tractor and "really trying it out."

All I could envision was the machine on two wheels whipping around in the fields, a wagon attached behind hitting whatever got in its way. Apparently my mom was thinking of the same thing or something even worse, because she told my father it was time to go. "And I'm driving," she said as they got into their vehicle and left.

Caution! Loaded question could backfire
July 8, 2010

This week my husband David and I celebrate our eighth wedding anniversary. I asked my beloved what he thought made our marriage successful up to this point.

His reply was, "I do what you tell me to."

I gave him a "who are you kidding" look and said "be serious just for a few minutes."

David sat quietly for a bit, I could see he was thinking hard about his next response.

"It can't be that hard to think of why we get along so well," I encouraged.

"You go first," my hubby said.

I was able to rattle off three reasons easily concerning our relationship. One, we laugh with and at each other. Two, David is ticklish and I'm not, and third, he's good at making a mess and I don't mind cleaning it up.

Not to be outdone, my spouse then whipped up three ideas of his own about our matrimonial reunion. One, I was willing to clean up animal poop and barf and he wasn't. Two, he was understanding about the way I redneck fixed things around our hobby farm and three, I was good at making fun of him and he was willing to let me.

Now the contest was on to see who could come up with the longest list of reasons why we got along so well.

I mentioned that it was really nice to be with someone didn't get mad when I spend more money on dewormer for my horses than I do on underwear for him.

David felt our getting along had to do with the fact that I didn't mind that he dressed up like a giant Whoopee cushion or beer bottle for Halloween. (I thought to myself, like I had a choice.)

I added to the list that we both liked cold pizza for breakfast, buying junk at garage sales we don't need and watching Pawn Stars on TV.

Three other common factors between us David noted include our love for animals, camping and fishing. "Even though we haven't been in years," he said sadly.

"That isn't my fault, I keep telling you to get the boat out, get it ready, pick a weekend and we'll go, "I said supportively.

"You're too busy and the cats turned the boat into a hotel," David sighed, "when I wasn't married I used to go all the time."

I gave my man a dirty look because over the years he knew I had asked him many times about going fishing. I even encouraged David to buy a male friend and go with him out on the lake. He always had an excuse why not to go and somehow I was connected with that excuse.

Now I was getting frustrated over my husband's little pity party and decided finding more reasons why I liked him had come to an end for the day.

Rapidly switching gears, David asked, "What do you want to do for our anniversary?"

"Go fishing," I replied.

"I can't have the boat ready by then. How about we go out for a meal?"

"Fine."

"Where should we go?"

"Somewhere that serves fish."

"You don't eat fish," David said rolling his eyes.

"That day I am."

""Now you're just being stubborn and unreasonable. How about-"

"Don't say anything else right now; I'm leaving to go spend time with my horses, alone."

A bewildered look passed over my sweetheart's face as he tried to figure out how a conversation went from praises to each other to the point where we were no longer in the same room.

I'm not going to try to explain it to him. He has many more years of anniversaries to work on that puzzle.

Hippie rode in on a bike, left in a Mercedes
July 22, 2010

His name is Skuzz, a long haired, 40+ year old man formerly from a hippie commune in California.

On a hot July day, he rode his bicycle to my parents' home located by a lake in northern Minnesota. The aged free thinker was on a mission to buy the 1973 Mercedes my father had for sale.

"Hey man," Skuzz asked, "could I please go take a dip in the lake? I'm really hot and sweaty."

"Sure" my father said, not knowing what else he really could say.

So Skuzz took off across the lawn, shedding clothes as he ran towards the lake. My mother was in their screened porch talking to her sister on the phone. She was unaware that Skuzz had come for a visit and was momentarily speechless at the scene unfolding before her.

"I have to hang up now Sister, there's a half naked man running through my flowers," my mom said.

"Is he cute?" my aunt asked.

"I don't know. I'll find out and call you back later."

As my father was walking into the house to warn my mother about Skuzz, he found her looking through a pair of binoculars.

"What are you doing?" he asked.

"The better question is, who is that and what is he doing?" my mother replied.

"That's Skuzz, he's here to buy the Mercedes."

"I hope he took his wallet out of his pants before he went into the water."

Skuzz appeared fifteen minutes later, dried off and dressed. He went through the perfunctory ritual of trying to purchase the car much cheaper than dad was asking for it. The two men haggled awhile longer before finally deciding on a price. Skuzz began laying out damp wrinkled dollar bills on the kitchen table.

"There," he said, "that should be all of it."

My mom counted the money twice then looked at Skuzz, "there's not enough here," she said.

The look on the hippie's face was one of genuine shock. He frantically fished around in his pockets looking for more cash. Not finding any he said, "I'll be right back," and dashed out of the house.

Returning only a few minutes later, Skuzz had the exact amount needed to finish the transaction. The deal was complete, so the man with unique past loaded his bicycle into the trunk of the car and left.

Mom and Dad watched the dust pillows left by the Mercedes and its new owner.

"Where do you think he had the rest of the money hidden?" my mother asked. "He was riding a bicycle, there's no ashtray on bikes to stash stuff."

"I don't think I want to know where he had it tucked away," my father said.

Mom and Dad sighed then smiled at each other. They were happy to have the little extra in their pockets for their upcoming trip to see the grandkids.

Mom picked up the phone and started dialing. My Dad asked her who she was calling.

"My sister."

"Didn't you already talk to her this morning?"

"Yes, but I told her I would call her back."

"Why?"

"She wants to know more about the recent entertainment in our yard."

"You mean Skuzz? What was so entertaining about him?"

"You didn't have the binoculars, so you wouldn't understand."

112

Trip to county fair completes summer
August 12, 2010

Summer is not summer without a trip to the county fair. How do you describe the combined flavors of cotton candy washed down with a cold one from the beer garden? The colorful screams of adults as they gamely accompany their ready-to-barf children on rides designed to permanently cross your eyeballs. And you certainly can't experience the true atmosphere of a fair until you walk through the hot, smelly hog and cattle barns.

Just a few nights ago my beloved husband David and I went to the fair. We were having a good time until he ate all my mini donuts. If you ask him, he'll say he bought them for himself and was sharing with me. I'm telling you that my spouse bought them for me and ate them when I wasn't looking.

"I can't believe you ate all my donuts," I said in frustration.

"You were busy taking pictures and the donuts were getting cold," David said.

"I'm not asking you to hold any of my food again!"

"Yes you will, as soon as you want to pet a rabbit or take a picture of something, you'll have me hold your corndog."

As it turns out, he was right (which he will be happy to see I admitted in print) because I just had to talk to and touch all the horses in the barn.

Of course you can't leave the fairgrounds without at least trying one of the games that very few people win at. We chose target shooting, the one where you have to shoot out the tiny star on a piece of paper four yards away from you. And of course, it's difficult to hold a pellet rifle with a slice of pizza in one hand and chocolate milk shake in the other. I handed David my supper and he promptly polished it off as I attempted to win a kid's bike.

Then he attempted to win a bike as I took photos of him, because of course, I had no food to eat.

113

There wasn't much time to visit the commercial booths or thoroughly enjoy all the exhibits; my sweetheart was in a hurry to get to…somewhere.

A short while later, an interesting photo op came along and Hubby needed to hold my hamburger and soda. They were gone by the time I snapped off three shots.

Before the torrential rain storm soaked our clothes and cheese curds, we managed to admire the bright lights of the carnival and smile at the happy sounds of people having fun. Delicious smells surrounded us and I realized then how much I love fair food. I just wish I had the chance to actually eat it.

Working through another manic Monday
September 2, 2010

My husband David is a firm believer that bad Mondays deserve a "redo." I agree with him.

His most recent Monday started off with the frustrating task of doing paperwork and making phone calls over an accident.

A week or so ago, while David was snoring deeply in his parked semi, another truck driver tried to back his rig next to my beloved and took out his side mirror. Ouch!

David's search for estimates had to cease though, when his favorite wife (that would be me) requested he help unload a 400 pound slot machine from the pick-up because her car had a flat tire and she had to go to work. (Don't ask about the slot machine, it is an unhappy subject between me and hubby).

Meanwhile, a veterinarian appointment had been made for one of our cats for the late afternoon. David said he would take the cat and the car and get them both fixed. "That's awesome of you Honey. Thanks," I said.

The day was going along pretty good for me when David calls. "The dryer doesn't work and I need clothes to go on the road tomorrow," he said.

"I told you last week the dryer wasn't working and you said it was probably just me."

"Well, maybe I was wrong."

"I know you're wrong. See if it's okay to take them to your mom's, I'm sure it won't be a problem," I replied.

"Okay" and my spouse hung up the phone.

A couple hours later and David rushes in to my place of employment and drops off lunch. "I'm on my way to the vet and I've got Isaiah with me," he said in a hurried manner.

"Why didn't you leave the dog home? It's hot outside."

"He wanted to go for a ride."

"Thank you for lunch," I said and rolled my eyes as he rushed out the door.

After an undetermined amount of time passed, David calls me again. "I'm broke down in Beroun, it's hot and I forgot my cell phone at home."

"Where are you calling from?"

"The gas station, the nice lady let me use the phone."

"I'll be right there," I said and rushed out to rescue the husband, cat and dog.

David dropped me off at work on his way home. He then went to get his father and the necessary equipment to retrieve the car. On his way back from getting the car, he and his dad stopped to pick me up from work. The car was dropped off at a local dealership to be fixed on our way home.

"I didn't get all my paperwork done and I forgot to buy milk," David mumbled.

I gave my sweetheart a hug. "What have you been doing all day?" I said in a teasing voice.

'Hoarders' not show for wannabe collectors
September 23, 2010

Back by popular demand…..

    So it seems anyway at the David Riedeman household. A small grumble was heard around Pine County a couple of weeks ago when I mentioned it was my last column in the Hinckley News. Apparently, reading about the escapades of my awesome, although sometimes unorthodox, husband provides a spot of humor for some of our neighbors. The man needs a certified fan club. It would keep him busy responding to emails instead of leaving half started projects on my living room floor.

    David's latest entertainment interest makes me nervous though. My beloved has started watching the TV show, "Hoarders." This program is one you watch with one eye open and one closed. Sort of the same concept when you drive by an auto accident, knowing it's not nice to stare, but hard not to. My spouse's enthrallment with the program has me wondering if he recognizes in himself the possibility of becoming a hoarder or he already is a covert one.

    I started thinking about it and soon images of David's stuff started playing through my mind like a bad "B" movie. There's a large slot machine on his crowded workbench that doesn't work, an apartment size stove in the pole shed that doesn't work, our old washing machine that, of course, doesn't work.

    Without having to look too hard, the broken, unused and unnecessary stuff quickly develops into a long list. A satellite dish we don't use, a TV antenna we don't use, a broken Bobcat, an old rusty hay feeder, old tires, a 30 year old broken snowmobile and boxes of mystery parts that belong to something nobody even has a clue about.

117

Then there's the big unspoken ugly, two riding lawn mowers each in about a hundred pieces in the garage space for my car. Now, I don't mind parking outside as long as there isn't snow on the ground. After all, I don't have a garage door opener. If I want the garage door open, I have to go inside the shop and push a button. When the fluffy frozen liquid arrives though, I want my car inside.

This list my not seem real long to you, but it's only a partial list. My fingers absolutely refuse to type any more words describing the junk on our homestead.

Now, I won't be a very honest person if I didn't admit that our property contains a few items that I could live without. I am perfectly capable of handing over clothes that don't fit, the extra Tupperware bowl, tablecloths that don't fit my table and music cassettes I no longer listen to. Hey, I certainly don't want to be accused of being a hoarder.

All in all, I can't complain too much about my sweetheart husband. He's a guy who likes guy things and thinks that "someday I may need that." Hmmm, in fifteen years you would have thought the purpose for what he needs it for would have arrived by now.

I'm afraid to suggest he go looking for it, because that means bringing the other half to our place and what if the two really don't match. If you think you have the other half to match what David has, call me, I personally deliver his half to you.

We can afford another dog
October 7, 2010

My handsome hubby David approved of another freebie this last weekend, very reluctantly I admit. Since we already have one dog, three chickens, four cats and four horses, he was not the first in line to approve of a new puppy. I know he was concerned his future might go on to include a miniature donkey in the garage or a milk goat operation.

"I have legitimate reasons for getting another dog," I told my spouse.

"There are no good reasons for getting another mutt," David grumbled.

"Yes there is. Want to hear them?"

"You don't need a good reason to have an animal, your father taught you that one," Hubby replied.

"True, but our dog now is getting older and –"

"Never mind the reasons. How much does the dog cost?"

"He's free."

"Nothing is ever free," David responded, "remember the cats and the horses? They've destroyed my wallet and they were 'free' too'."

"You're exaggerating. Besides, you love them and you know it," I said while flashing him a sweet smile.

David didn't respond he just kept driving to the place where the next KoodB Ranch member was currently residing.

After we picked up the puppy, I set him on my lap, his face towards David. It didn't take long before our adorable addition blinked his big brown eyes at my beloved. David then slid into the spirit of finding a name for him. The process soon became a hilarious game as the names ranged from family members, Norm or Ed, to friends Frank or Bill, to ridiculous attention getters like "Pig or Riedeman."

We finally settled on "Windsor," David's favorite beverage besides Kool Aid.

Deciding on a name was the easy part, the first night home with the little guy was not. I had forgotten that a baby is a baby no matter the species. That means at ten pm, midnight, two am, four am and six am he wanted to play, eat and poop. During the entire disturbance, I dealt with the emotions of our other dog and cats, which ranged from "what did you bring into this house" to "okay, I maybe like this little guy."

I must add that while David grumbled a lot about Windsor, he also was the first one to buy him toys, pick out the collar and officially give him his name. My sweetheart handed me the camera after barely getting home so that I could take photos of Windsor. Those photos he promptly emailed to friends and co-workers. And while he was acting the proud papa part, I was laying down puppy pads so Windsor wouldn't have an accident on the carpet.

As I watched David lay on the floor and play with the puppy, I commented, "I know you said that since I wanted the dog, I had to be the one to take care of him, but how come you get to enjoy the benefits of our new cutie and I have to do all the work?"

"It's that way with all our other pets now, why should this be different?"

I couldn't think of a good response so I picked up my camera and started taking photos of my big tough spouse letting Windsor sleep on his tummy The next time he says he doesn't like animals, I' have pictures to proof otherwise. And I'm not afraid to use them.

Drug haze inspires conspiracy theory
October 21, 2010

I have great respect and admiration for the nurses and medical attendants who have ever been assigned to my husband David's care. It takes a tremendous amount of patience to deal with a man who thinks that medical professionals plot to send him to the morgue.

Most recently, my beloved was assaulted by the terrible pain brought on by a kidney stone. David was headed south on his normal truck run when symptoms indicated that he had better turn around and head for home. By the time he reached Wyoming, Minnesota, David could go no farther and stopped at Fairview Medical Center. He was admitted right away and that's when the fun began.

As soon as David received his first dose of "going to my happy place" medication, his misplaced paranoid feelings let loose like puppy diarrhea.

"They are out to get me. Someone wheeled me down to a room with a small dark tube and made me lay down in it, I think it was a coffin," David said in a whisper.

"Nobody is interested in sending you to the morgue honey. That tube is called a MRI; it's just a giant X ray machine."

"I almost got stuck in the tube, it was scary."

"I'm sure you didn't almost get stuck," I said to David as I retied the size small hospital gown on my size extra-large husband.

"I think they want to off me," he said in a voice heavily influenced by a necessary prescription, "they stick needles into me, make me drink lukewarm broth and don't offer enough TV channels to choose from."

I tried to be gentle when responding to David's concerns. After all, he wasn't feeling well and the medication was definitely causing his brain to short circuit. Just a couple of hours earlier he was doing the waltz with his IV machine up and down the hospital hallway.

"Not only are you exaggerating Honey, but what benefit would it be to nurses to kill off their patients? Then they would be out of a job."

David didn't seem to have a comeback to my comment, so he tried to focus on spearing Jell-O with his toothbrush. I heard him mumble something about a conspiracy, but didn't quite get what he was saying.

Once my sweetheart was home, I was relieved to hear him say how impressed he was with the staff at Fairview Medical Center. He even called them up and told them how he felt. There were no comments made about torture, morgues or twelve inch needles.

I figured the follow-up visit at our local clinic should be uneventful. No so, people in the waiting room were laughing because my husband decided to make announcements concerning the necessity of me being in the exam room. Apparently, David wanted it known that I was his witness in case someone tried to hurt him. I informed him that I was the only one interested in volunteering for that task.

Send hubbies to housebreaking boot camp
November 11, 2010

After having conversations with several wives, I came to the conclusion that I should start a boot camp for husbands.

The same themes of frustration seem to reoccur during our chat sessions and the main question among most of the women is "how do I fix his behavior?" (Take note men: the ladies mentioned your behavior, not your personality.)

That got me thinking since I am married to one of those men who need a bit of refinement in the practicality and motivational aspects of day-to-day living.

My husband David is awesome and I love him dearly, but he still needs an occasional butt kicking. When it gets to the point where he's leaving beard shavings and nail clippings in my sink, because he doesn't want to dirty his sink, it's time for a refresher course.

The first aspect of the camp is its location. I'm thinking of a self-contained compound in the middle of the Sahara Desert.

Sneaking out at night for a beer run would be pretty impossible. Cell phone, television and internet services would be unavailable. The mail service will not be delivering "Golf Digest" or "Dune Buggy Delight." That's not to say the men won't have entertainment available to them. I'm pretty sure they're capable of creating a game using a dryer sheet and radishes.

It's expected the guys will go through sports and reality TV withdrawals, so I'll furnish the rooms with marshmallow guns and Doritos. The bedrooms will have bunk beds so the male species can have their own "fart out my roommate" contests. As for bathrooms, I'll go with the RV design where the shower, toilet and sink can be hosed down, with or without the husband in it. If this doesn't sound like a place where males will be training to learn how to improve their wives' lives, have patience, there is a method to my madness.

Guys wanting clean underwear or towels will have to pick the dirty items up off the floor, walk 50 steps to a laundry room and learn how to use a washing machine.

At some point, leaving everything they own on the bed, counters and floors will create a panic among the men as they attempt to find their personal jerseys for a game of pineapple football.

Once they can no longer lie on a couch or sit in a chair without the dirty socks of fifteen men draped on the furniture, a small aha seed will start growing between their ears.

If I had my choice, the guys would have to hunt and gather their own food, prepare it and hand washes the dishes afterward. I'm sure it would be difficult to find venison in the desert, so I'll settle for the husbands making meals for each other from cans, boxes and jars.

When the males grow weary of eating with their fingers, they will figure out that dishes have to be washed; counters have to be cleared off and wiped down. When they are tired of their bare feet sticking to the dirty floors, the floors will get mopped.

In the next segment of this column, we will be discussing decision making and choices that don't make wives want to buy one way tickets to Greenland.

Husbands refrain from phonee baloney
November 25, 2011

In a previous column I talked about a boot camp for husbands. Since I didn't receive any death threats in regards to its contents and my husband David didn't serve me with divorce papers, I'll forge ahead with part two of my column.

It is a wonderful thing that our husbands love us and want to be near us. How flattering that they enjoy our company and refuse to leave our sides. So what's the problem?

As much as we the ladies appreciate our husbands' attention; being followed throughout the house and asked, "Where ya going and whatcha doing?" on a constant basis builds a frustration in a woman that no amount of chocolate or shopping can cure.

There needs to be a happy medium between husband and wife spending time together and the ladies being able to open a closet door without eyes peering over her shoulder.

It makes me laugh when I hear of men who spend a weekend in the woods with one match and granola bar; yet the minute they walk in their home, can't sit on the couch or fix microwave popcorn unless their wife is right beside them.

I'm refining the details on how this issue will be handled in husband's boot camp, suffice to say, I'm always open to suggestions from other wives.

The next topic to be addressed has to do with phone calls. The spectrum is wide, ranging from the male spouse who never calls his wife to the husband that calls every hour asking, "whatcha ya doing?" Usually when David calls every hour he gets a standard response, "Same dang thing I was an hour ago when you called." Now he spaces the phone calls to two and a half hours apart.

Somebody (preferably a woman) needs to invent a device that can be installed on the phones of husbands who actually call too much. Every time the spouse tries to call his wife, the phone doesn't work. As for the men who don't call their wives enough, a device (also invented by a woman) could be put on their phone that automatically calls the wife at times predetermined by the wife.

Okay, so a husband's boot camp sounds a little far-fetched, but it doesn't hurt for a woman to dream about options for her beloved, does it?

And men, this is not a pick-on-you column; this is a fun reminder format instead of a nag-because-you-deserve-it. We all know that husband/wife relationships are complicated, hysterical and perfect fodder for columns. Right now all I can do is hope my husband learns to wipe his running nose on a handkerchief instead of a dishtowel.

Bungled birthday forgettable
December 9, 2010

After my last birthday, I'm not sure I want another one. I don't say that because of the wrinkle increase, the memory decrease or paying AARP dues. There wasn't the expectation for flowers, fireworks or a surprise anything either. No, I just wish that the mishap I encountered on my birthday could have happened on a non-birthday day.

The morning of my birthday I went to check on things at the home of family who had gone on vacation. Their driveway was deep in snow so I parked on the road. I left the car running for two reasons; one, I was only going to take a few minutes to do the chores and two, it was cold outside and my car needed to warm up some more. Proud of myself for remembering the car remote after locking the car, I took off to do what I needed to do. Much to my surprise when I returned to the car, the remote didn't work. Oh crap, now what? I did what I always do when in trouble; I call my resourceful husband David. Fortunately, my cell phone was in my coat pocket.

After explaining my dilemma David says, "Why did you lock the car in the first place?"

"I told you why."

"Why don't you unlock it using the keypad?"

"Because I never use it and I don't have the number memorized. It's written on a piece of paper in my purse which is locked in the car."

"Good place for it," David snickered. "I'll call Norm and see if he remembers the number." (We bought the car from David's brother Norm several years ago.)

My spouse called me back several times that morning with the wrong keypad number. Meanwhile, David also called a friend that lives a half mile down the road from where I was.

(The plan was for the friend to take me home so I could get the spare key.) The friend said he'd be right there.

After fifteen minutes the friend hadn't shown up. David calls his house again and the wife said he left right away. We find out later that he mixed me up with someone else's wife and went to her house.

I called one of my friend's not too far away and she said she would also be right there. That is after her 96 year old father was done with his business in the bathroom. Oh boy, that ride will be awhile coming.

Finally, the right keypad number was delivered and I was able to get in my nice warm car. It was recommended I tattoo the number somewhere on my body. The response to the suggestion as you can imagine, is unprintable. To add insult to injury I was late to work and forgot my lunch.

I would like to say that my beloved hubby gave me a birthday present that made those unpleasant situations seem trivial. He didn't, David gave me a box of chocolates and a used wheelchair. And that is another whole story in itself.

2011

Thanks to handy, helping hubby
January 6, 2011

Be careful what you wish for.

I used to dream about having someone to help out while I worked at an outside job. A person who would cook, clean, run errands and keep the husband out of trouble.

This last week, my husband David was home for nine days. He was looking forward to some rest and relaxation, I was looking forward to having that someone to help prepare for the upcoming holidays.

The first item on the agenda had to do with the unfinished Christmas gifts. I had an idea for what I was planning to give, but had decided if time didn't allow for me to make them, I'd go shopping.

David took charge and set up my embroidery machine and the 100 spools of thread in my living room.

"Why don't you embroider in the hobby room," I asked my beloved as I watched our cats take off through the house with various strands of thread in their mouth.

"There's no TV in the hobby room," David replied as he balanced a large bowl of popcorn and equally large glass of pop on an unstable TV tray. Both dogs were sitting next to my honey's feet looking at the popcorn with lust in their eyes. As I walked out the door, I tried not to envision what the house would look like when I got home from work.

The next day my spouse decided to make candy, hot dish and meatloaf. I was very grateful for all the leftovers for work, but wondered if the dirty dishes that filled the counters, kitchen table and bathroom were worth it.

"Couldn't you have cleaned up a little bit?" I asked while scrubbing sticky candy cane off the floor.

"I did. I loaded the dishwasher once and prepared the garbage," David replied.

"Did you run the dishwasher?"

"No, not yet."

"And what do you mean by "preparing the garbage?""

"I tied the garbage bag ends together so it's ready to take out.""

"But you didn't actually take the garbage out of the house, did you." I said while taking my sweetheart's four sweatshirts off the kitchen chair.

"No, not yet."

Once again I surveyed David's handiwork, and was thankful the refrigerator was full and the food ready to go for a potluck despite a kitchen that looked like it belonged on the "Hoarders" show.

A few presents still needed to be wrapped and I told David I would take care of that item on the "to do" list. But like he had been all week long, my other half insisted that my time at home needed to be spent with him, "enjoying each other's company, not always working."

Okay, so while I sit next to David on the couch watching "Ice Road Truckers," there are still gifts waiting for cheery holiday wrapping paper and a trip to the post office. On that same "to do" list is laundry, addressing the last of the Christmas cards and cleaning a house that went from livable to can't find anything.

I will admit that the man I live with did vacuum once, did clear a space on a kitchen counter and did fold a basket of clothes. These things do not go unnoticed or unappreciated. It just would be nice if the vacuum had been put away, the space on the counter had been wiped down and the basket of clothes hadn't been piled with tools from the shop.

Anyone that knows me always knows that I have been bragging to people about David's rescuing me during this holiday season. He really was a lot of help while I was at work. I just wish his rescue had been a tad less messy.

Old dog up to same old tricks at obedience class
January 20, 2011

It's training time at the Riedeman household. And no, I'm not referring to my husband David. After almost nine years, he understands the program around our place, most of the time anyway.

These next few weeks it is Windsor, our four and a half month old puppy that's headed for obedience school. He needs to learn the commands sit, stay, heel and down. (I know I said David didn't need training, but it still wouldn't hurt for him to pick up a few helpful hints.)

The night of the first lesson arrives and Windsor, David and I are there on time. Several large dogs and their owners are calmly walking around, warming up for the class. Windsor the smallest and youngest dog there promptly tucks his tail and hides under the folding chairs.

"Get him out from under those chairs," David said.

"I'm trying, "I tersely replied as I struggled to untangle gangly limbs and a long tail from the cold metal legs of a chair. My beloved was too preoccupied taking photos to help.

Windsor's first day at school needed to be immortalized. So while I worked to convince my very frightened puppy that what we were doing was fun, David took lots of pictures of wagging tails and yapping snouts.

Half way through the session I asked hubby if he wanted to work with Windsor.

"No, you're doing just fine," he said, "Besides, Windsor doesn't like me."

I had to wait until I had walked another full circle back to David before I could respond to his comment.

"He likes you just fine; you just don't want to walk in circles to get some exercise."

On my next trip around, David said something I couldn't hear because he had the camera in front of his face.

Again, I had to walk the full circle before I could ask my honey what he had said.

"I said, Ssshhhh, the instructor is talking, pay attention to what you're doing."

Pay attention? This sentence is coming from a man who needs an activity book during the church service so he doesn't talk.

There was also a pattern happening with David and the camera. I would hear the sound of the shutter click after I had walked past him, not as I approached him. That meant he was taking butt shots of me. Oh boy, I was not happy about that.

I ignored my spouse and continued with my puppy training mission. It didn't take too long for Windsor to understand what was expected of him. By the end of the session he was doing quite well. That is when I decided the dog was getting the treat when we got home, not my husband.

Bedroom color hot topic
February 17, 2011

Renovation – a bittersweet word promising newness and disaster.

Such it was at the Riedeman household when we decided to paint our bedroom, steam clean the carpet and rearrange the furniture. The first issue of disagreement was deciding on the paint colors.

My stylish husband David would have black walls and orange trim if it was his choice. I told him I would not live in a perpetual state of Halloween.

Instead, I picked out a dark green for one wall and a cream color for the other three walls. These colors matched the wallpaper border I had purchased four years ago. My spouse, noticing the official color of the green paint, began to make jokes.

"Oh boy, now I can tell people we're going to have a hot bedroom because the paint color is called "Jalapeno."

I tried to ignore David, but when he started telling everyone in the hardware store that we were going to have a hot bedroom, I threatened to take away his bag of candy if he didn't stop. Unfortunately, the jokes took a different direction when my sweetheart began mimicking a well known puppeteer and his "Jalapeno on a stick" puppet.

I swear I though David was going to somehow find a Mexican sombrero to buy. The man would be sleeping on the couch if he didn't quit chanting "I'm going to have a Jalapeno on a stick bedroom."

Speaking of sleeping, the only place available to put our mattresses while the bedroom was being painted was on the living room floor. My dogs and cats thought this was a great idea since it instantly provided one giant pet bed for them.

Our painting and carpet cleaning project was not able to be completed in one day so we had to share our mattresses with our "babies."

David grumbled quite a bit when our bobble head 40+ pound puppy wedged himself between us. He really got upset when two of our cats decided to wrestle at the end of the mattresses at 3 a.m.

Me, well pretty much anything animals do is cute, so a rough paw on my head or cat tail around my neck is okay with me. When the furniture had finally been put in its new locations, David and I discussed the finishing touches for our bedroom.

"Are you done with the quilt you started four years ago for the bed," my husband said in a mocking tone.

Knowing full well it was one of those projects I had only barely started, I in return asked him, "Are the closet shelves and additional clothes pole put up like you said you'd do four years ago?"

David was quiet a moment before responding with the question, "Wouldn't a dance pole be fun in our bedroom?"

I wanted to believe I didn't hear him right, but I knew I had. "Will you wrap your thighs around it and swing on it?" I asked in all seriousness.

"I would if I could," Hubby responded, "but my belly's too big and I'd get pole burns on it."

"Exactly," I said, "ditto for me."

Caution! Objects may appear larger through bifocals
March 10, 2011

To see or not to see, that is the question. Actually, it's more of a statement of fact concerning my beloved husband, David. He was complaining that he couldn't see up close with his current pair of eyeglasses.

I said to my spouse, "You probably need bifocals. You're about the age when most people start needing a little help in that area."

David ignored my comment and his situation until one day the hard truth stared right at him.

"I can't see the numbers on my cell phone," he whined, "I've been calling wrong numbers for the past week. So far I've talked to people at a urology lab, bridal shop and the FBI."

"Could be worse, I teased him, "at least you didn't call a psychic network."

I decided not to make David feel worse by letting him know that his not being able to see clearly had caused a few problems at home too. Mostly small incidents like putting folded clothes in the wrong places. Kitchen towels in dresser drawers and underwear in the kitchen towel drawers, horseradish instead of mayo and chocolate syrup instead of maple syrup on pancakes.

When my honey nearly left the house with my purse instead of his briefcase, that's when he decided it was time for a new pair of glasses. Even if my purse is large and heavy, he should have noticed the bright blue color.

After David had his eye exam, it was time to pick out eyeglass frames. This event is on the same level of fun as cleaning a chicken coop or paying taxes. David's mind still lives in the 80's which means so does his taste in fashion.

It's bad enough when he wants to wear dress shoes with sweat pants, but his choice in eyeglass frames becomes almost frightening. My man really thought an extra large pair of black

137

plastic frames, like Buddy Holly's, looked good, maybe on Buddy Holly, but not my husband.

David also considered a dark purplish red frame. He said it would be less boring. Maybe so, but it also made him look like Elton John. I was afraid every time I looked at him the song "Rocket Man" would be stuck in my head.

We finally settled on a pair of eyeglasses, ordered them and anxiously awaited their arrival.

Unfortunately for David, they came in on a day I had to work. He went to pick them up, bringing our two dogs with him. Guess he figured that if he had too much trouble with the new glasses, at least he'd have a couple of dogs that could lead him around.

Since this was David's first pair of glasses with bifocals, the lady at the optical department reminded David to move his eyes and not his head while getting used to them.

"But don't move your eyes too quickly, you might get dizzy." My sweetheart was also warned, "That objects can appear closer than they really are."

David replied, "Don't worry, all I have to do is make it to the pickup and then I can drive." Watch out Pine County.

When I asked my other half how he was doing with the new glasses he said, "Not bad except for the high stepping when I come to a curb. I didn't know my knees could touch my nose. So far the only bad incident was when I was reaching for something on a store shelf and almost grabbed the lady next to me."

Oh boy, I'm a little concerned my wonderful David won't be seeing things the way he should at home. Of course, I sometimes wonder how that is different from any other day.

Husband enters next stage of life – retraining
March 24, 2011

Which is easier, training or retraining? Our seven month old puppy Windsor is in the training stage of life, my husband David, is in the retraining phase of life.

Last Sunday, Windsor and our older dog, Isaiah, were left in the house for a couple of hours while David and I went to church. We didn't want to be late for the service so we hurried out of the house without going through the usual checklist.

This list entails putting all edible items on top of tables, counters or inside cupboards. Included on the list are wastebaskets, any food even if already packaged, boxes of tissue, anything inside of anything else and furniture.

Before church actually started, David handed me his service bulletin and asked me if he could see mine.

"What's wrong with yours?" I asked.

"Here, you'll see," he said with a grin that meant he definitely did something wrong.

I looked inside David's bulletin and found two scratch off cards and all the silver coating that was once on them.

"Are you kidding?" I hissed, "You rubbed scratch off tickets in church?"

My hubby ignored me and stared instead at what once was my bulletin.

I had just enough time to leave the pew, go to a garbage can and clean my bulletin before the service started.

About the second hymn, my spouse leaned over and whispered, "I forgot to put away the meatballs I made this morning."

"Well, you better plan on making some more when you get home. If Windsor can reach them, he'll eat them."

More than he usually does during a service, David rolled his eyes, played with whatever was within arm's reach and squirmed in the pew. It was not because of the singing or message, but because he was upset over the fact that Windsor probably ate his pound and a half of meatballs.

When we returned home, we were not surprised to see the puppy had spread garbage all the over the house, put mud prints on the bedspread and, of course, ate the meatballs.

As David walked out the door to go to the grocery store, he asked me several times, "Do you need anything else?"

"No."

"Are you sure?"

"Yes!"

"Okay, I'm not going back to the store again," he said firmly.

"I don't need anything!"

My beloved made a trip to the grocery store for hamburger while I cleaned up the rest of the mess and the dogs went outside.

A couple hours later, when it came time to make the sweet and sour sauce for the meatballs, I heard a loud "oh no" come from the kitchen. (He didn't actually say "oh no," but I won't say what he actually said.)

"What's wrong?" I asked.

"I don't have enough lemon juice for the sauce," David said in a frustrated tone of voice.

"Didn't you figure out what all you needed before you started?" I tried not to giggle, but it was just too difficult.

David just gave me "the look" and headed back to the grocery store.

All I can say is "Amen, Lord, Amen."

Birthday wishes include black jelly beans, beer
April 14, 2011

I'm pretty excited about summer arriving in the next couple of months. Nine months of snow or mud and three months of flowers and sunshine; it doesn't sound fair, but I'll take it. Only a couple more snowstorms (you know they're coming) before we can trade boots for flip flops and long johns for bikini tops. (Not me of course, I don't want to scare the loons.)

I have a decent sized list of projects I am looking forward to tackling when the weather remains somewhat warm. My outhouse needs painting, fences re-enforcing and there is still lots of dog poop to clean up after the lakes in my yard somewhat dry up.

This week though, is special. It is a time to celebrate no matter what the weather conditions. My hubby David turns 45 on April 14.

He claims his age is a much younger number and I agree. There are times when it is difficult to believe he is a middle-aged man.

It is actually easy for me to create a long list of awesome attributes about my man. For starters, he is kind, considerate, generous and intelligent. He allows the puppy to sit on his belly and the cats to walk on the computer keyboard. The flowers he gives me from the grocery store are the best available and David would never be the responsible party for an unused vacuum.

We all have our "pebble in the shoe" traits that irritate others and David is no exception.

I think my honey's favorite number is half. He finishes half his projects, eats half of what I try to hide from him and is right half the time. The glass is either half full or half empty, depending on the situation.

Although David appreciates any gift given to him, it's still not easy to buy for him. Socks, underwear and tee shirts are boring gifts year after year. A trolling motor is too expensive, books are definitely out of the game and tools are well, tools.

My sweetheart likes orange shag carpet and black velvet paintings. His favorite foods include pickled eggs and ultra-hot salsa. David likes watching cartoons, fishing shows and "The Price is Right."

If I could afford it; I would arrange a chartered fishing trip with Bob Barker as the captain for my beloved. Since David doesn't eat fish, the galley would be filled with steak, black jelly beans and his choice of beer. I would give him new rods, reels and fishing gear, but not the wish for me to parade around in a tiny swimsuit.

Happy Birthday Honey! I love ya!

Hard to tell trash from treasure
May 5, 2011

I undertook a rather frightening project this weekend, cleaning our basement.

The place had become a nightmare with its totes of Christmas decorations, boxes of mismatched Tupperware and garbage bags of clothes that no longer fit.

I asked David for help, but he said he was too scared.

"Are you sure you don't have time to help me go through our stuff?" I asked.

"No Honey, sorry, I've got my own list of things to do."

"Like what?"

"Umm," my spouse paused before saying, "I need to clean the chicken coop and grease the tractor.

"What about getting rid of all the unneeded stuff in the basement?"

"Get rid of anything you want except my things," David said as he made a stop at our couch, laid down on it and started watching an obscure movie on the inside of his eyelids.

"It's probably better I clean the basement myself," I mumbled to myself, "My sweetheart might decide to start saving beer bottle labels."

Some interesting realizations came to mind as I packed up at least 25 of my hubby's baseball caps. My spouse needs that many caps. He leaves one in every room of the house, every building on our property and every vehicle we own. So why does he have to ask me where he put his hat?

One of David's other collections overtaking the basement is jars. He has accumulated enough jars for canning the fruits and vegetables of every garden in Pine County. It would be nice if we had a vegetable garden, but apparently Mother Nature has decided to vacation on another planet and let Minnesota become a state with the four seasons of winter, winter, winter and whatever.

I also discovered in the far corners of my basement, treasures. Items I thought I had lost or at least misplaced for a long time. I didn't even know I had a beach umbrella. Of course, in those far corners were also spiders, cob webs and indefinable objects. Ish!

While David enjoyed his silent movie, I sorted through the pantry area of basement. Behind the juicer we haven't used in six years, I found a kit to make your own dog biscuits and a bottle of chocolate wine. Chocolate wine?

By the end of two days I realized I don't need two totes of purses, a two-wheel shopping cart or a plastic policeman cookie jar. I also don't need boots in which one was eaten by the dog, ten year cable bill statements or small squares of Styrofoam. I really don't need a blender with only one working speed, bottles of expired hot sauce or coffee cans of small parts to something David took apart in 2006.

The List: Guide to family reunion
June 16, 2011

Due to a family reunion at our home next month, I created **THE LIST** to help me and my husband David prioritize the items that need to be done.

The problem is what I consider priority and what my spouse considers priority. For me, it's the food menu, providing comfortable sleeping arrangements and entertainment for the kids.

It's not that these items aren't important to David; it's the questionable choices he picks out for each category.

On **THE LIST** where is says "stock basement refrigerator and buy food," my hubby came up with his own interpretation of the words. He thinks an old painted toilet sitting in the front yard filled with ice and beer not only takes care of the beverage situation, but is perfectly suitable décor. Add a wheelbarrow full of potato chips, hot dogs burnt over a fire pit and the food part of the party is taken care of.

Also included on **THE LIST** is set up the tent for the kids, put out the holiday decorations and repaint the outhouse. David is still unsure about the necessity of the tent for the impending relatives. There are three things concerning the tent he is worried about. The grass turning yellow where the tent is pitched, the games played in the tent and the hours it will take to repack it into its 12 inch square nylon envelope.

"Look," I said to my beloved, "I'll help you set up the tent then you inflate the air mattresses to put inside it while I find pillows and blankets."

"The kids don't need air mattresses," David whined, "they're tough. Give them a piece of cardboard and a sleeping bag."

I gave my sweetheart the smile that meant, "Do as I say before I hurt you."

145

In my opinion, decorations are one of the funniest parts of planning for a party. I like fountains, my hubby doesn't. He says the sound of the running water makes him want to pee. I like wind chimes, my hubby doesn't.

Apparently the noise puts the image of Tinkerbell in his brain and he finds it difficult to think of anything else for days. I like holiday signs, candles and tacky jewelry. My spouse likes special holiday liquor, cookies and the reason to consume both.

Neither David nor I are "game" people. We prefer to visit with people rather than fall on our faces doing a potato sack race or strain our brains guessing the name of some obscure politician from Rhode Island. I did strongly express to my honey though, that we need to have available a couple of activities for the visiting nieces and nephews.

"How about we divide the kids into two groups and see which one can pull the most weeds from my garden in a 20 minute time limit?" David suggested.

"Umm, I don't think the children will like that game," I said slightly irritated, "We need to set up the volleyball net and horseshoe pit."

Of all the preparations on **THE LIST** for the family gathering I think David enjoyed painting the outhouse the most. He had the biggest smile on his face while he stenciled "Riedeman Resort" on the outhouse door and hung holiday toilet paper from a nail.

Hubby can't live without retro mobile
July 21, 2011

It started with a phone call from my husband David. A while back he was at a garage sale and wanted me to meet him at it because he found something "I couldn't live without." This really means, I can live without it but he can't.

"You need to hurry up at get here," my sweetheart urges, "other people are looking at it too."

As I drove to meet my beloved, I thought about the many possibilities of "it." It could be anything from an incomplete mechanical do hickey to well used furniture from the 1970's, David favorite era.

I was barely out of my car when hubby started babbling excitedly about a $300 Cadillac that he thought would be perfect for me.

"It needs a little work, but it runs," he said, "and we need to start seriously looking for a replacement for your current vehicle."

What I saw before me was a car the size of the Titanic with large rust holes in its side. I looked inside the car discovering an interior that may have been on the bottom of a large lake.

"What do you think?" David asked. "We can always replace the door that has holes in it, but it might be a different color."

"You called me away from cleaning bathrooms for this?" I replied as nicely as possible, "It's too big. I'd need a mile of airport runway to park it."

My spouse was disappointed, especially since he'd always wanted an older, ocean liner size Caddy.

It was about a month ago since David tried to convince me to purchase that sinking ship Cadillac. Then the Caddy curse struck again. Just down the road from us another Cadillac came up for sale. It was newer than my sweetheart's previous find. It's reminded me of a vehicle needing a pair of Longhorn steer horns.

My other half is thoroughly convinced that this "the one;" the car that fits all my needs.

"Look how big the back seat is, both dogs will fit comfortably back there. And see the huge trunk? Lots of room for all the crap you carry around."

"It has leather seats," I said. "I'll stick to the seat in hot weather and the dogs will puncture holes in it."

"We'll get seat covers," David replied.

I had to admit the car was nice. The trunk was huge, even big enough for one large husband. It had electric everything and a dashboard like a NASA spaceship. Then I discovered the selling point for me, a small feature on the rearview mirror that displaced the direction as I drove. For someone directionally challenged like me, this was almost as good as having a chauffeur.

We decided to buy the 15 year old Cadillac. The day we picked it up, my love was as excited as if he'd just purchased shag carpet and lava lamps.

We drove to town for fuel and a car wash. As we were going through the car wash I sat in the luxurious passenger seat admiring various features of the car. By the time the six minute wash was over I was wet. Seems the Caddy of the husband's dreams had a major windshield seal leak. At least the trunk stayed dry. *(Sigh.)*

Take me out to the ball game
August 4, 2011

I wasn't sure what to expect. Some close friends of mine had invited me to a Twins baseball game at Target Field. Not only was it my first Twins game, it was also my first live baseball game (if you don't count my children's T-Ball games 20 years ago).

Hmmm, what do I wear? What necessities do I need in my backpack? My husband David will also be accompanying me, what do I need for him? A leash? A tracking device?

As always I over packed, figuring I should be prepared for any situation. By the end of the day I knew I didn't need to bring a first aid kit. I mean 90+ an hour flying baseballs and breaking bats, did I really not think medical personnel would be plentiful? I didn't need to bring a sweatshirt; the weather had been hot enough to give the devil boils. I didn't need to bring bug spray, hair spray or items to entertain my spouse.

There were four of us that loaded up into our vehicle and headed for the twin cities; men in the front seats, women in the back seats. I settled in and looked forward to an enjoyable road trip with Hubby and friends.

My beloved is a long haul truck driver so I assume he always knows where he's going and the best way to get there. This, I found out, is not true. I for one do not say a word about how to get somewhere since I was born directionally challenged. If I didn't have the small letters on my rearview mirror that displayed the N,S, E, W, etc. I'd be in trouble. After much "discussion" between the occupants in our vehicle, we agreed on a place to park. It turns out it was several blocks from the stadium, but what the heck, walking never hurt anyone (except a member of our party experiencing leg pain).

I figured the traditional foods; hot dogs, beer and soda would be available to purchase. I had no idea I would have more choices than an international food convention. Various brat flavors, Asian cuisine, Mexican and Italian, who would have thought so many options at a ball game! So what tasty treats did I end up eating for a meal? I consumed a hot dog, a corn dog, M&M's and a can of root beer. What can I say; I'm a traditionalist food junkie.

It's not always a good idea to follow the crowds, but when I saw 2/3 of the baseball crowd wearing some type of Twins clothing, I just had to blend in. So the hunt was on for a woman's tee shirt, not too expensive and a style that made me look slim. I ended up with a garment that met two of the three requirements, that was the best that about 45 vendors had to offer.

I had brought my camera with the extra-long lens, hoping for some awesome action shots. It was unfortunate the game was not riddled with home runs, slides or a fight. Don't get me wrong, I thoroughly enjoyed watching it and hope to see another one soon. Yet there was some disappointment I wasn't able to capture an image worthy of Sports Illustrated.

I've never been much of a sports fan unless it involved horse racing. After a day of happy fans, intense ball playing, fabulous food and fine friends, I am a now a devoted Twins fan!

Can't catch a fish with a wish
August 18, 2011

My husband David wakes up one weekend morning and wants to go fishing.

"Yea!" I said.

"The boat is already packed with life jackets and fishing poles from the last time we used it," my sweetheart says.

Excellent. I gather up a few other items we'll need: a small cooler of drinks, extra clothing (in case the weather gets bad or one of us falls in), a bag of snacks and my personal bag containing camera equipment and everything else except the kitchen sink.

Meanwhile, Hubby is outside collecting worms. He informs me after 20 minutes that he couldn't find very many.

"We live on 10 acres Honey, how can you not find enough worms?" I ask.

"You must give them all to the chickens."

"We have three chickens and I do not take the time to hunt and feed worms to them."

David decides to stop at a gas station on the way out of town and buy worms. Fine with me. For a $1.50 it's worth not listening to my spouse complain about the low grub shortage. It's a perfect day to be out fishing; warm sunshine, a light breeze and a lake with only one other boat on it. We drop anchor in a corner of a small bay.

My love says to me, "Okay Honey, get the fishing rods out." I look in the storage compartment next to me.

"Not in this side, they must be on your side."

David digs around in the storage compartment on his side.

"They're not here, you're sure they're not on your side?"

"I'm sure; it's pretty hard to miss a group of four fishing poles."

My spouse is unhappy. He's not sure who took the fishing rods out of the boat or where they might be. As he mumbles about them maybe being put in the camper by my crazy relatives, I'm laughing hysterically because what else is there to do. You bring bait, food, supplies, a tackle box and then no way to catch fish unless you do it using your hands or a net.

Tucked in the dark corner of another compartment David finds a collapsible cane pole. I think it's great and encourage him to use it. We're already out on the boat; we have hooks, store bought worms and red licorice, "give the cane pole a try," I tell him.

It took him a little bit to master the coordination of the cane pole. The first fish landed in my bag, the second fish hit me in the back of the head and third one left a slimy imprint on David's hat.

An amazing thing happened that afternoon though. David caught fish, enough sunfish to feed his parents. He even admitted that he was having fun. Once in awhile he would comment that he wished he had a rod and reel. I quickly reminded him that the three guys fishing in the other boat weren't catching anything.

"Besides," I told him, "I needed a good laugh today and there's no doubt you landed a big one in that category.

Husband no mule skinner
September 29, 2011

One bright and glorious morning my husband David said, "Let's go for a ride."

"Sounds great," I replied.

The four of us - me, David and the two dogs piled into the pick up and went to his parent's place. They have 80 wooded acres with lots of trails perfectly groomed for walking.

My honey, I soon found out, did not have walking in mind. He said it would be more fun to go on the trails riding in his folk's "mule." (The mule is a small four wheel drive vehicle with no sides and a short sided bed on the back.)

"Walking would be good for us," I said sweetly as I tried to convince my husband of the benefits.

"Nah, not this morning, the ground is too wet and we didn't bring boots."

He had a good point and I mentally kicked myself for not planning appropriately. There's nothing worse than soggy socks and tennis shoes. I hate trying to peel them off my feet, small rocks and pieces of other unknown substances left clinging to my toes.

So we took off in the mule, me and David in the front seat, our older dog Isaiah riding in the back and our younger dog Windsor running alongside.

I watched for photo opportunities as my spouse happily drove down the first trail. An unpleasant event, one that would continue to repeat itself, soon occurred. Branches, still wet from the rain the night before, brushed against me. I clutched my camera close to my body to keep it dry while I was whacked by drenched shrubs and maple tree leaves. Occasionally, tiny bugs would find their way behind my sunglasses and globs of Windsor's drool would fly up and land on my bare arms.

Somehow David didn't seem to suffer from the causalities of our outing. His smile started at one ear and ended at the other. His clothes weren't nearly as damp as mine and I couldn't see anything else sticking to him except remnants of his breakfast.

Just when I didn't think it could get worse, one of the swamps lay before us like a pit that goes straight to the bowels of earth itself. With only one hand available, I wrapped my arm around one of the roll over bars and started praying really hard.

When you mix hubby, mud and a four wheel drive together, you can forget about sanity. I wasn't even worried about getting covered with mud as I believed the swamp would swallow us whole like the giant cockroach in the movie "Men in Black."

Much to my relief, we didn't disappear in the swamp. In fact, hubby somehow figured out my nervousness of the situation and decided to detour at the last minute. Maybe it was the screaming or threats of sleeping on the couch that gave away my feelings.

I was slapped in the face only a couple of times by tree branches on the way back to his parents. My photography opportunities consisted of taking four pictures of spider webs glistening in the sunlight before Windsor ran through them.

When we got home David said he going to take a little rest before starting his next project. I didn't even ask what was next on his list, I just mumbled that I needed to go change clothes and find my rubber boots.

About the Author

Tami found the magic of words in the fifth grade. It started with poetry and went from there.

She and her friend Dona from Napa, California co-authored two fictional novels; *The Golden Road, French Wine or Moonshine* and *The Golden Road Detour*.

Tami and her husband David, currently reside on their hobby farm, KoodB Ranch in Sandstone, Minnesota.

Besides being an award winning columnist, Tami is also an award winning photographer.

For more information about Tami Jo Riedeman, her books and photography go to her web site at: www.koodbcreations.com.

Order Form

Book	Price	Quantity

☐ Yes, My Love Muffin...............$14.95 ea _____

☐ The Golden Road,...................$15.95 ea _____
French Wine or Moonshine

☐ The Golden Road Detour...........$15.95 ea_____

Prices include shipping and handling

Mail check or money order (no cash please) to:

KoodB Creations
P.O. Box 614, Sandstone, MN 55072
320.260.5735

Check out my website:
www.koodbcreations.com